BEASTLY NEIGHBOURS

BEASTLY NEIGHBOURS

WRITTEN BY MOLLIE RIGHTS

ILLUSTRATIONS BY KIM SOLGA

CAMBRIDGE UNIVERSITY PRESS
Cambridge
New York   New Rochelle
Melbourne   Sydney

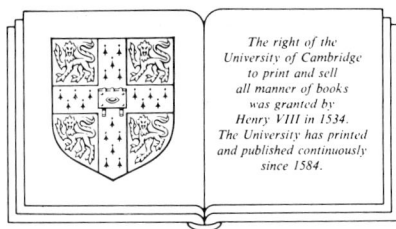

Published by the Press Syndicate of the University of Cambridge
The Pitt Building, Trumpington Street
Cambridge CB2 1RP
32 East 57th Street, New York, NY 10022, USA
10 Stamford Road, Oakleigh, Melbourne 3166, Australia

Printed in Great Britain by Scotprint Ltd, Musselburgh,
Scotland

British Library cataloguing in publication data
Rights, Mollie
[Beastly neighbors]. Beastly neighbours.
1. Urban fauna – Great Britain – Juvenile literature
2. Urban flora – Great Britain – Juvenile literature
I. Title   II. Solga, Kim
508.41   QH137

ISBN 0 521 34268 6 hard covers
ISBN 0 521 34809 9 paperback

The publishers would like to thank Anglian Water for their
help with 'Where does the rain go?'

WHAT'S IN THIS BOOK?

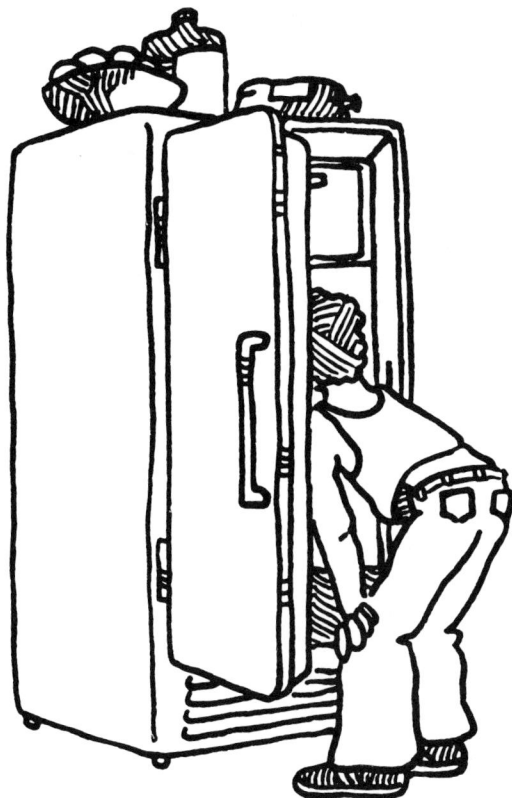

Nature is wherever you are. It's under your feet, over your head, and just outside your door. It's even inside your fridge. You don't have to walk miles to visit a tree, study an ant, or gather seeds for a windowsill garden. You can feed the birds, build a pond, and grow wildflowers even if you live three flights up in a high-rise building.

This book is about exploring the wild world around you. The activities, expeditions, and experiences in it are for wherever *you* are, whether you live in a rambling house in a suburb or in a high-rise building in a town. So read this book and meet your beastly neighbours.

CONTENTS

1
WILD IN THE SUPERMARKET

We see some of our beastly neighbours every day: they look out at us from the refrigerator or pop up in the supermarket, and we eat them for breakfast, lunch, and dinner. They don't really *live* in refrigerators or supermarkets; they began their lives outdoors just as most plants and animals do.

Tonight when you have supper stop to think about what you're eating, about what you're *really* eating. Are you chewing on leaves, seeds, or roots, or on the wing muscles of a bird? If that sounds a little wild and primitive to you, it should. All our garden plants were once wild. Just because you buy tomatoes in a supermarket all wrapped up in plastic doesn't mean your tomato isn't a berry. It even has ancestors that still grow wild in the mountains of South America.

Roots, Fruits, and Leaves We Eat

When is a vegetable a fruit? When most of us think of fruit, we think of sweet ones such as cherries, apples, and bananas; yet many fruits aren't sweet at all. Fruit is the name we give to the part of a plant that has seeds inside. It's called the "ovary." Cucumbers and green beans are two of the nonsweet fruits we eat. Usually we call them "vegetables," but "vegetable" is a general term for all or any part of a plant. Fruits are vegetables, but not all vegetables are fruits.

Cabbage, carrots, and turnips are not fruits. You can probably name at least five fruits we eat that aren't sweet: green peppers, aubergines, garden peas, pumpkins, tomatoes, okra, avocados.

Some of the food we call "seeds" are really fruits too. Corn, wheat, and other grains are fruits. In these the ovary is thin and sticks to the seed. Sometimes we throw away the ovary and eat the seeds. Dried beans and white rice are two such foods. Can you think of five other seeds we eat? (Walnuts, almonds, sesame seeds, peanuts, peas, and baked beans.)

Underground Edibles

Did you ever think about running away from home to live in the woods and wonder if you could really live on roots and berries? Even Stone-age people didn't live only on roots and fruit. They fished and hunted deer and other wild animals. But roots and other underground plant parts were very important to them, and they still are important to us. Before people had refrigerators and before lorries were available to carry food from warmer parts of the world to colder parts in winter, underground edibles were important. They fed people during the winter when leaves, flowers, and fruit weren't available.

Carrots, beets, and turnips are common roots we eat. Don't be surprised if you didn't know carrots are roots. Lots of people don't. Some people even think carrots have tiny seeds inside. (They don't. It takes two years for a carrot plant to make seeds, and then it doesn't make them in

its roots. The first year it grows a root and some leaves. The second year it makes a tall flower stalk and beautiful white flowers.)

FLOWERING CARROT

When Is a Root Not?

The potatoes and onions we eat, although they grow underground, aren't really roots. They are special parts of the plant used for storing food. The onion stores its food in a bulb. At the base of the bulb is a flattened stem; each layer of the onion is a thickened storage leaf.

The potato stores its food in an underground stem called a "tuber". Each eye of the potato is a bud for a new stem, which can produce a whole new potato plant. When a farmer wants to plant potatoes, he or she plants pieces of potato instead of seeds. You, too, can do this.

HOW TO GROW YOUR OWN POTATO

1. LOOK FOR A POTATO THAT HAS BEGUN TO SPROUT A LITTLE.

2. CUT IT UP SO THAT EACH PIECE HAS AT LEAST TWO BUDDING EYES.

EYES

3. PLANT EACH PIECE IN A POT OF SOIL. EACH PIECE SHOULD GROW INTO A NEW POTATO PLANT.

4. IF YOU WANT YOUR PLANTS TO GROW NEW POTATOES, THEY WILL NEED MORE ROOM THAN A POT CAN PROVIDE. AN OLD PLASTIC BUCKET, WASTEBASKET, OR AN OLD TYRE WILL DO FINE. PUT DRAINAGE HOLES IN THE BOTTOM.

5. GROW YOUR PLANTS WHERE THEY GET LOTS OF SUN. KEEP THE SOIL MOIST BUT NOT WET.

11

Roots in the Sugar Bowl

You may not like the idea, but you probably eat a lot of roots. And you don't have to eat turnips and beets to do it. If you eat cake, sweets, and ice cream, you are eating roots. But you won't know it from reading the ingredients on the package. The secret is in the sugar.

Some of our sugar comes from stems, that is, from sugarcane. But a lot of it comes from a special kind of beet called the "sugar beet". These beets don't

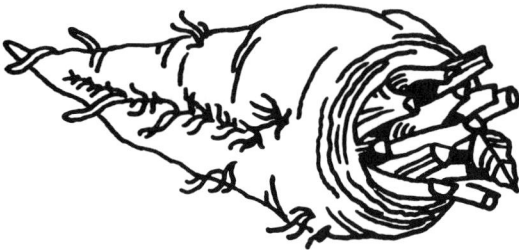

look like the red beetroot we eat. They're white, for one thing, and very large. You can't tell whether your sugar comes from beets or cane by tasting it because chemically they're the same. Sugar beets grow in some parts of the British Isles, while sugarcane grows in tropical places such as Hawaii and Brazil.

Digging for Fruit

Underground seems like a strange place for a fruit to form, but that's exactly where peanuts grow. At first glance peanut plants look rather ordinary. They have green leaves and yellow flowers. The flowers bloom above ground the way all flowers do, but once the flowers are pollinated, a strange thing happens. The flower stem begins to grow and bend toward the ground. It keeps growing downward until it has pushed the ovary holding the seeds into the soil. Once underground several centimetres the peanut seeds grow and develop inside their ovary shell.

If the peanuts are grown commercially, they're dug up by a machine when they are ripe and left in the sun to dry for a few days. Then another machine comes along and picks the peanuts off the plants.

12

FIND THE PLANT IN THE PEANUT

1. TAKE A PEANUT SEED AND SEPARATE THE TWO HALVES.

2. AT ONE END YOU'LL FIND THE TINY LEAVES AND ROOT OF THE NEW PLANT.

(NOTE: ALTHOUGH ROASTED PEANUTS WON'T GROW, YOU CAN STILL SEE THE TINY PLANTS IN THEM.)

An Apple a Day

An apple begins as a flower that blooms and attracts a bee. The bee flies from blossom to blossom collecting nectar and pollen. Pollen is the male part of the flower. Apple blossom pollen sticks to the bee's hairs as the bee crawls over the blossom. When the bee lands on another flower, pollen from the first flower is dusted onto the female stigma. Then the pollen begins to grow a pollen tube. The tube

HOW TO PLANT PEANUTS

TO GROW YOUR OWN PEANUTS YOU NEED:

RAW PEANUTS FROM THE SUPERMARKET (ROASTED OR SALTED ONES WON'T GROW)

USE STERILIZED POTTING SOIL OR BLACK, CRUMBLY SOIL FROM OUTSIDE.

PLANT POTS FILLED WITH SOIL. PAPER CUPS AND EMPTY MILK CARTONS MAKE GOOD PLANT POTS. PUNCH HOLES IN THE BOTTOM FOR DRAINAGE.

1. TAKE THE PEANUT SEEDS OUT OF THE SHELLS AND SOAK THEM OVERNIGHT.

2. PLANT TWO OR THREE SEEDS IN EACH POT. SOME MAY NOT SPROUT.

3. PUT THE POTS IN A SUNNY SPOT. WATER THEM REGULARLY, BUT NOT TOO MUCH. CHECK THE SOIL WITH YOUR FINGER TO SEE THAT IT'S DAMP, NOT SOGGY.

4. WHEN THE PLANTS BEGIN TO GROW, PULL OUT THE EXTRAS, LEAVING ONLY THE HEALTHIEST ONE IN EACH POT.

ANYONE CAN GROW PEANUT PLANTS, BUT IN ORDER FOR YOUR PLANTS TO MAKE MORE PEANUTS THEY NEED LONG, HOT SUMMER DAYS, LOTS OF SUN, LOTS OF SOIL.

IF YOU LIVE WHERE SUMMERS ARE LONG AND HOT, PLANT YOUR PEANUTS OUTDOORS IN THE SPRING WHEN THE WEATHER GETS WARM. SEEDS CAN BE PLANTED RIGHT IN THE GROUND IF THE SOIL IS RICH AND CRUMBLY, OR YOU CAN USE LARGE PLANTPOTS AND POTTING SOIL.

grows down into the ovary, which is where the seeds will grow. There it fertilizes an ovule, which will grow into an apple seed.

Soon the petals fall off the apple blossom, but the sepals under the petals stay on. You can still see them when the apple is ripe. Meanwhile the apple begins to grow. It gets larger and larger and finally is full grown. Depending on the kind of apple, it will turn red or yellow or stay green when it's ripe. Finally it's ready to be eaten. If the apple tree grows in your garden you can pick an apple and eat it right away.

In the old days we could buy apples only from late summer through winter. They were available when they were getting ripe on the trees and before the last winter apples spoiled. Now you can buy them all year round, thanks to cold and controlled-atmosphere storage.

You Leaf-Eater, You

Caterpillars chew away at leaves, and people do too. Lettuce and spinach are just two of the many leaves you can find in a supermarket. (There are brussel sprouts, watercress, kale, cabbage, basil, and parsley, to name a few.)

Sometimes we eat just the leafstalk, not the leaves. Celery and rhubarb are two examples.

Celery has compound leaves. Each leaf has many small leaflets on it. Every leaf has a bud at its base, but the leaflet parts of a compound leaf don't. Where are the leaf buds on a celery stalk?

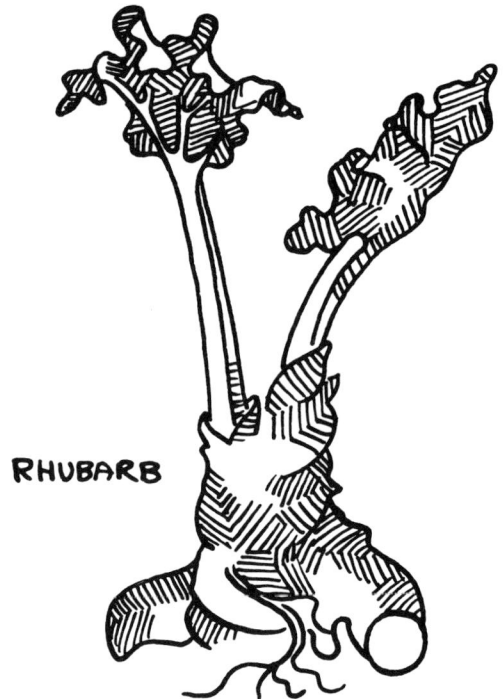

RHUBARB

All plants drink water to grow and stay healthy. When a plant is growing in the ground, it takes water through its roots. Plants can also drink water with their stems and leafstalks. We put cut flowers in water so they can drink and live for a while without their roots. You can see how a plant drinks if you watch celery stalks placed in coloured water. The colour shows you where the water goes in the stalk.

HOW TO DRY APPLES

IF YOUR OVEN HAS A PILOT LIGHT, YOU CAN DRY APPLES IN IT. YOU NEED A PIECE OF ALUMINIUM WIRE MESH THE SIZE OF YOUR OVEN'S SHELVES.

1. USE PLIERS TO TURN THE ROUGH EDGES OF THE WIRE MESH SCREEN UNDER TO PROTECT YOUR HANDS.

2. LAY THE WIRE SCREEN ON THE OVEN SHELF.

3. SLICE THE APPLES VERY THIN (YOU CAN LEAVE THE SKINS ON). ARRANGE THEM ON THE SCREEN SO THEY DON'T OVERLAP.

4. CLOSE THE OVEN DOOR AND TAPE A NOTE ON THE STOVE SO NO ONE WILL TURN THE OVEN ON WHILE YOUR APPLES ARE DRYING.

STOP APPLES INSIDE

5. DRYING TIME DEPENDS ON HOW WARM YOUR PILOT LIGHT MAKES THE OVEN BUT WILL PROBABLY TAKE 4 TO 8 HOURS, OR OVERNIGHT.

OUTDOORS

APPLES CAN BE DRIED OUTDOORS, TOO, BUT IT TAKES LONGER. YOU NEED A HOT, SUNNY SPOT AND TWO PIECES OF WIRE SCREEN. SLICE THE APPLES ONTO ONE SCREEN AND COVER THEM WITH THE OTHER TO KEEP AWAY INSECTS. TURN THE APPLES ONCE A DAY UNTIL THEY'RE DRY.

NOTE: HOME-DRIED APPLES ARE SUPPOSED TO TURN BROWN. THEY WILL BE MUCH TASTIER THAN COMMERCIALLY DRIED FRUIT, WHICH IS TREATED WITH SULPHUR FUMES TO KEEP IT WHITE.

WATCH CELERY DRINK

1. PUT A FEW DROPS OF RED OR BLUE FOOD COLOURING INTO A GLASS OF WATER.

2. CUT THE BOTTOM OFF A FRESH CELERY STALK THAT HAS LEAVES ON IT.

3. LET YOUR CELERY DRINK FOR SEVERAL HOURS, THEN CHECK TO SEE WHERE THE COLOUR IS BY CUTTING ACROSS THE STALK.

Flowers Good Enough to Eat

Flowers are beautiful; they smell nice, and some are good to eat. Usually we like to eat them when they are in the bud stage, before they have actually bloomed. Broccoli is an edible flower. Can you think of another? (Hint: Part of its name is the word "flower.")

Wild Plants

The plants we grow for food have changed a lot since people have been growing them. In the past they've been selected and bred for size, colour, tenderness, sweetness, and keeping quality. You can imagine what our plant ancestors looked like by thinking small and by looking at their relatives today and by watching the plant itself go to seed. A lettuce plant going to seed, for example, gets tall and thin. The flower stalk has just a few small leaves, and they taste bitter. A flowering lettuce looks a lot like its wild relatives.

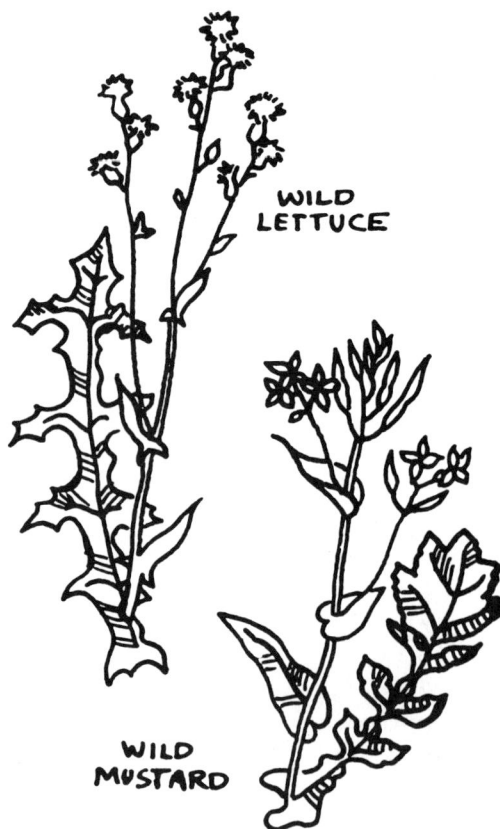

WILD LETTUCE

WILD MUSTARD

16

Tomatoes still grow wild in the mountains of South America. The plants look like cherry tomato bushes, and the tomatoes are tiny, red berries.

Peas are relatives of wild sweet peas; artichokes are relatives of thistles; and broccoli and cabbage are relatives of wild mustard.

Mechanical Tomatoes

People are always changing the plants they grow. Plant breeders now select plants that can be harvested by machines. Tomatoes are a good example. When people grow tomatoes in their own gardens, they want large, sweet, juicy fruits with tender skins. They like to pick a few tomatoes every day, so it's best if they don't all get ripe at once. Tomatoes like these have to be picked by hand because they'd be smashed by a machine, and green ones would be picked along with the ripe ones. Because it's very expensive to harvest commercial tomatoes by hand, special tomatoes have been bred for machine harvesting. They are medium size, firm bodied, not too juicy, tough skinned, and all ripen at once. They are tough enough to take machine handling, but they aren't as sweet and juicy as the old-fashioned kinds.

The Grasses You Eat

When you eat a slice of bread or some rice, do you think of grass? All of our grain plants, such as rice, oats, wheat, and rye, are grasses. Even maize is a kind of grass. Wheat and oats still look a lot like their ancient relatives. Maize, on the other hand, has changed a great deal. No one is certain what the first maize plants looked like.

17

HOW TO SPROUT SEEDS

ALFALFA SEEDS AND MUNG BEANS ARE THE MOST COMMON SPROUTS, BUT YOU CAN ALSO SPROUT WHEAT AND OTHER GRAINS. GROCERY AND HEALTH FOOD SHOPS HAVE MANY KINDS OF SEEDS YOU CAN TRY.

1. SOAK THE SEEDS IN WATER OVERNIGHT.

2. DRAIN OFF WATER AND PUT THE SEEDS ON A WET PAPER TOWEL ON A DISH.

3. KEEP THE TOWEL WET UNTIL THE SEEDS SPROUT.

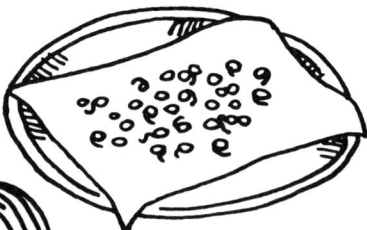

4. EAT!! SPROUTS ARE GOOD ALONE OR IN SANDWICHES, SALADS, AND SOUP.

CLOTH OR NET HELD ON WITH A RUBBER BAND

USE A SPROUTING JAR IF YOU GROW A LOT OF SPROUTS, THEN YOU DON'T NEED THE PAPER TOWEL. RINSE THE SEEDS WITH FRESH WATER EVERY DAY. IF YOU WANT GREEN SPROUTS, SET THEM IN THE SUN.

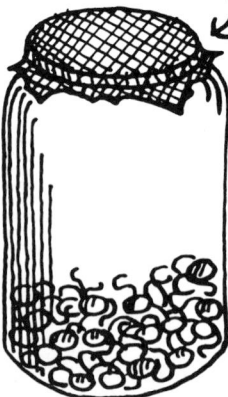

CAUTION: SOME SEEDS INTENDED FOR PLANTING MAY BE TREATED WITH CHEMICALS. BE SURE THE SEEDS YOU SPROUT ARE INTENDED TO BE EATEN AS SPROUTS.

The Flowerpot Farm

You can be a farmer, no matter where you live. You need a little sun, a little water, some containers, some seeds, and some soil.

Sun. Check your windows windowsills, doorstep, garden or roof. Don't be discouraged if you don't have much sun. Some plants don't need direct sunlight if they get plenty of light.

Containers. Large-size milk cartons with the tops cut off are great. Flowerpots are okay too. Be sure your containers have holes in the bottom for drainage, so the roots won't get water-logged and rot. Put a saucer underneath to catch the extra water.

Most strawberries are grown from small plants, which you can get at a nursery but you can also get seeds for alpine strawberries, which grow very well in pots.

Soil. Sterilized potting soil, which you can buy at a nursery or gardening shop, is best, but you can also use ordinary soil. Try to find soil that's black and crumbly because it will have the minerals and texture plants need.

Water. Most people water their plants too much. Every day you should feel the soil around your plants. If it feels dry, add water. If it feels damp, don't water it.

Seeds. You can grow any seeds you have in the cupboard. Dried beans, whole peas, popcorn, and *raw* peanuts will grow in pots. Peas and beans will even flower and produce a crop. Corn and peanuts need more room to grow up in, but there are many other plants you can grow to harvest size in pots. Here are just a few: parsley, coriander, lettuce, Tiny Tim tomatoes (need sun), basil (needs sun), mint, chives, and strawberries (need sun).

Buy your seeds at a nursery or gardening shop or order them from a seed catalogue.

Fertilizer. Liquid house-plant fertilizer will help your plants grow. Wait until they are several inches high before you use it, then follow the directions on the bottle.

Growing the Groceries

Plants from your refrigerator can be grown for decoration the way house plants can. In many cases you can eat most of the plant, then grow the rest.

Carrots, beets, turnips, parsnips. Use the top inch or the whole root. Cut the leaves back leaving just a stub. New leaves will soon grow. Plant in potting soil in milk cartons or large cottage cheese containers. (Do not forget to make drain holes.)

Sweet potato. If you live near a large market, you may sometimes see sweet potatoes for sale. Use the whole potato. Sweet potatoes are sometimes treated to keep them from sprouting. To find a sweet potato that will grow well, look for shiny purple bumps on it. The new shoots will grow

20

from these buds. Plant in a jar of water with half the sweet potato submerged. Support it with toothpicks, or use a jar with a small mouth.

Avocado stone. Wash stone. Grow it in a jar like the sweet potato. The *flat* end goes down.

Pineapple tops. Pull the lowest leaves off the top. Then let the whole top dry out for a day. Plant in soil. A cut-off plastic washing-up liquid bottle makes a good container.

Hairy Roots

Root hairs look like bristles on a bottle brush, but most people never see them. When roots drink water from the soil, they absorb most of it through tiny root hairs. When carrots and other roots are pulled out of the ground, these delicate hairs break off. You can see what they look like by sprouting seeds in the dark. Bean seeds are good for this.

HAIRY ROOTS

1. SOAK THE BEANS OVERNIGHT.
2. SUPPORT THE BEANS IN THE JAR WITH DAMP BLOTTING PAPER.
3. COVER THE JAR WITH FOIL OR A LID.
4. PUT THE JAR IN A DARK CUPBOARD OR DRAWER.
5. CHECK THE JAR EVERY DAY. IN A FEW DAYS THE ROOTS WILL BEGIN TO GROW AND YOU'LL SEE THE ROOT HAIRS.

Muscles, Large But Not Tough

Most of the meat we eat is muscle. You already know at least a little about muscles; you have quite a few yourself. You know that some people have big muscles to start with and that anyone can make his or her muscles bigger by exercising.

Flex your arm and feel the muscles change shape. Every move an animal makes is controlled by muscles. Usually two muscles work together. Your triceps shortens and extends your arm, while your biceps relaxes and gets longer. To flex your arm, the opposite happens—the triceps relaxes and gets longer while your biceps shortens and pulls up your arm.

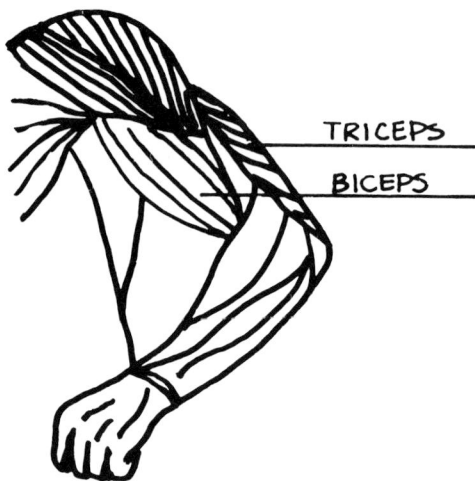

Because we eat muscles, farmers are interested in breeding animals that have large, but not tough muscles. Cattle, pigs, chickens, and other meat animals have been bred over the years to have large, tender muscles. We don't want our meat animals to develop their muscles through exercise because it would not only make them larger, it would make them tough.

The tenderest meat comes from young animals that have not exercised their muscles much. Tender veal is from calves, for example, and we prefer to eat lamb because sheep meat, or mutton, is strong flavoured and tough.

Where to Find a Steak on a Bullock

It's not too hard to figure out where a steak on a bullock comes from, at least in a general way. Imagine you're a bullock. You have nice meaty muscles all over your body. Now trot around the fields a bit. Remember that the muscles you use *least* will be the most tender. They will become the steaks. On all animals the tenderest muscles are along the back, an area the butcher calls the "loin." On a bullock this is where T-bone and porterhouse steaks come from. When you look at a T-bone steak, you can see a cross section of the backbone. From farther back on the bullock come less tender cuts, such as rump steaks.

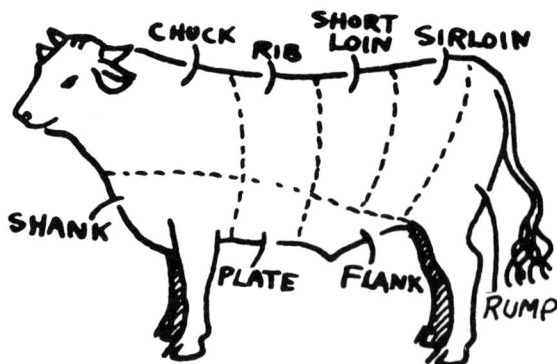

Legs have the toughest meat. A lot of leg meat is sold as mince or stewing steak. Cuts that are used for casseroles come from high up on the leg toward the back. Meat from above the front leg is called "chuck". Chuck steak is tasty but can be tough so chuck is often made into casseroles and stews.

The heart is one of the hardest working muscles an animal has. This should tell you something about how tender it is to eat. Take a good look at a heart the next time you're in a butcher's shop. Beef hearts usually aren't sold in one piece, but pig's and lamb's hearts are. These hearts work the same way that yours does.

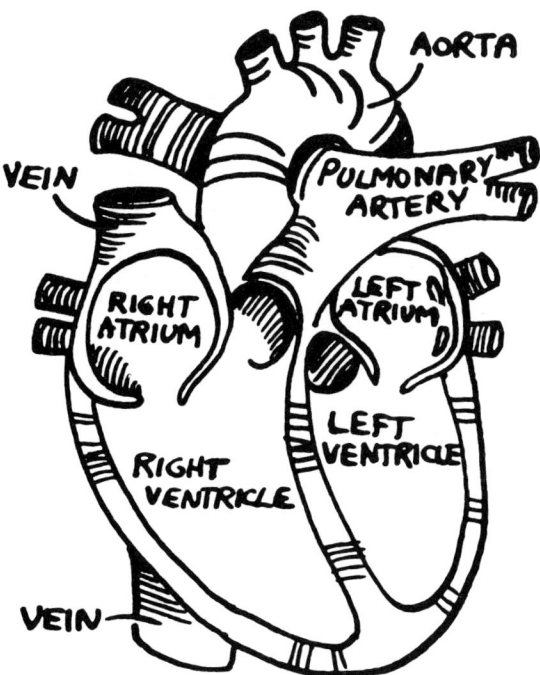

Pigs

Tender pork roasts and chops come from along the back, just as tender beef is along the back. Spare*ribs* are easy to figure out. Hams are from above the rear leg, and hands come from above the front leg and often have the bones removed. That's easy, but what about bacon and salt pork? These two pieces are cut from the side after the ribs have been removed for spare-ribs.

You can remember it this way: A pig runs with its feet, using the muscles of its hams, hands and springs. When it lies down on its side, it rests on its ribs and bacon.

Tuna fish

It's hard to imagine that the tuna in the can was ever a beautiful fish, silvery and large. There are several different kinds, but most canned tuna is yellowfin. These fish are caught in huge purse-seine nets.

All tuna are frozen whole as soon as they are caught. Tuna

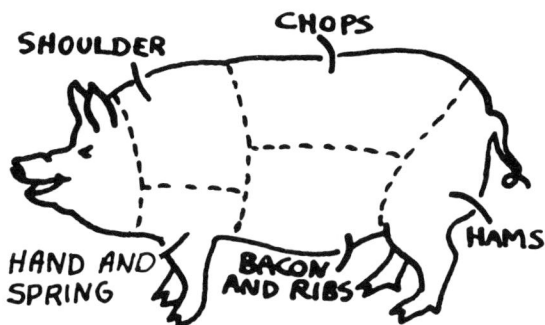

YELLOWFIN

ALBACORE

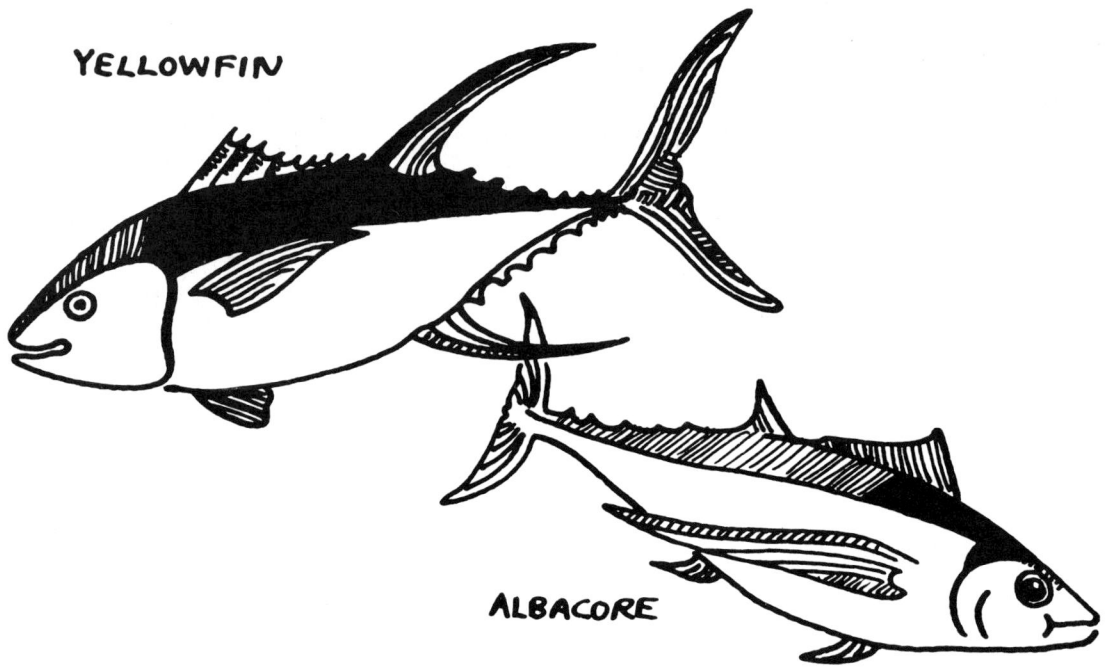

are usually sold directly to the cannery, where they are first cleaned, then cut up and canned. The scraps go into pet food.

Clams

Clams are sometimes called "shellfish," even though they aren't really fish at all. Clams, oysters, and scallops are molluscs. All molluscs have soft bodies, and most have a shell covering of some kind. Besides having shells, clams protect themselves by digging into mud or sand or by living under rocks. They have two tubes called "siphons," which reach up through the sand to the water. One siphon brings water down to the clam so the animal can take oxygen from it with its gills and filter small plants and animals

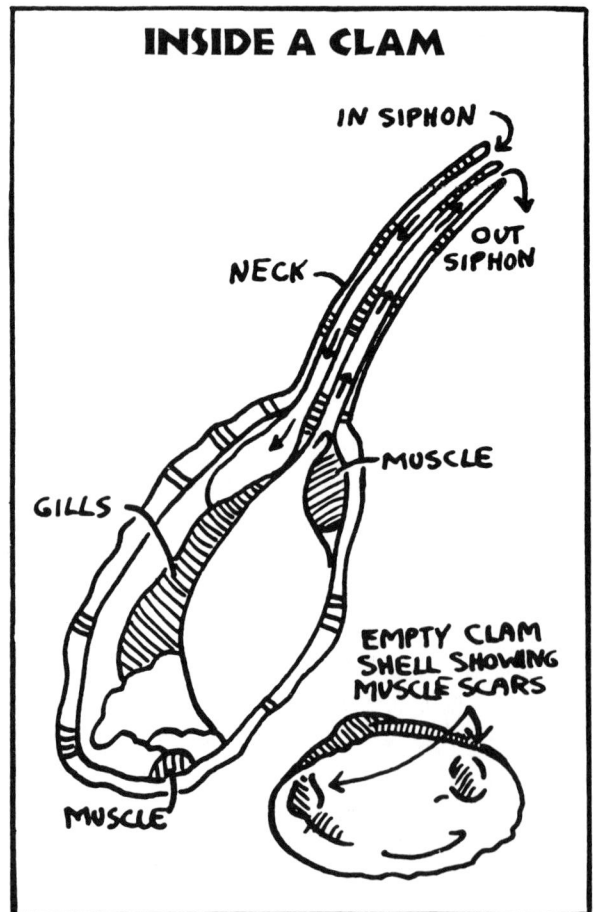

INSIDE A CLAM

IN SIPHON

OUT SIPHON

NECK

MUSCLE

GILLS

MUSCLE

EMPTY CLAM SHELL SHOWING MUSCLE SCARS

from it to eat. The other siphon shoots the "used" water back to the surface. In most clams these two siphons are joined together. They form the part people call the "neck." The next time you see a clam, look for the neck, the gills, and the frilly edges of the mantle. If the clam is still in its shell, you can see the muscle scars where the clam's muscles attach to clamp the shell closed. Clams are good at clamming up because their muscles are very strong.

An Oyster's World

Oysters don't dig their way into the soil the way clams do. Instead, they fasten one of their shells to a rock or other hard surface. This makes it difficult for a predator to prise the oyster loose and eat it. Commercial oysters are grown on old oyster shells, which can be picked up easily by special dredges. Unfortunately, this also makes it easier for other predators to eat them as well. Some oyster farms grow their oysters on strings that hang down into the water from platforms or rafts. This keeps the oysters off the bottom and out of the reach of some of their predators.

An oyster begins its life when sperm from a male oyster and an egg from a female oyster meet in the water. Since meet-

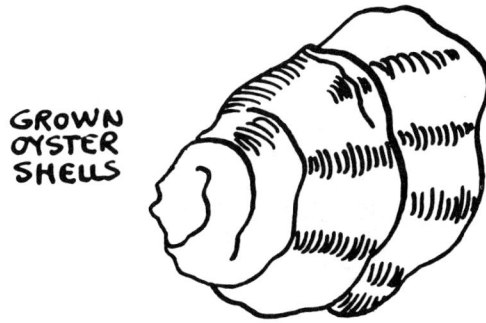

GROWN OYSTER SHELLS

BABY OYSTERS

ing in the water is a risky business, oysters have to release millions of eggs and sperm to ensure that enough will meet. At first the new oyster doesn't look anything like its parents and is so small you can see it only with a microscope. The first days of its life are spent swimming and drifting in the water, where it may be eaten by one of many other animals. And, eventually, when the water temperature and other conditions are just right, it will settle on some hard surface and begin to look more like the oyster we know.

While an oyster is growing up, it risks being eaten by stingrays, starfish, and oyster drills (marine snails). Once grown, it's ready to be eaten by us.

Do you ever wonder what your chances are of finding a pearl when you eat an oyster? A pearl is formed when an oyster is irritated by something that has entered its shell, something such as a small parasite or grain of sand. To protect itself, the oyster covers the irritation with pearly layers of the same material it uses to line its shell. Unfortunately, this doesn't happen very often. Only about 1 in 1,000 oysters has a pearl. Most jewellery pearls come from special pearl oysters, which are grown in Japan.

Scallop Jets

When we eat a clam or oyster, we eat the whole animal, but the scallop you buy in the shops is only part of the animal. The part you eat is the large muscle the scallop uses to close its shell.

Scallops live on the ocean floor. To escape from enemies such as the starfish, the scallop can move by using a jet-propulsion system. Jets of water are shot out when the scallop, using its large muscle, clamps its shells together. The water jets zip the scallop away through the water and away from its enemies.

A scallop is special in another way. It has many beautiful blue eyes, which peer out when the animal sits with its shell open. Perhaps it's just as well we eat only the scallop's muscle.

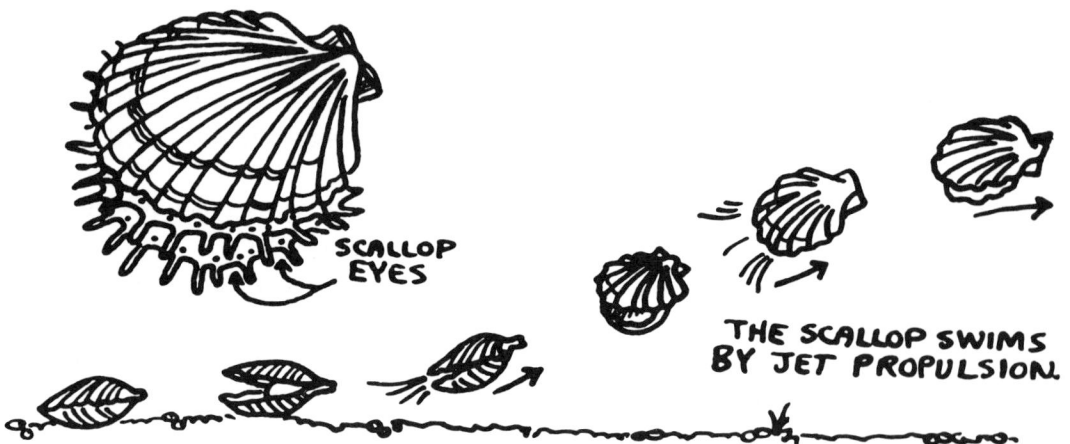

SCALLOP EYES

THE SCALLOP SWIMS BY JET PROPULSION.

26

The Story of Stone Soup

Stone soup is easy to make because it's made with whatever is around.

The story of stone soup begins with three soldiers who were out of money and very hungry. They were on their way to a town, but they knew that the people were not fond of soldiers and would probably hide their food rather than share it. On the way into town one soldier picked up three smooth stones. He asked the first person he saw in town if he could borrow a large pot,

explaining that he had some good soup stones and was going to make soup. The person was suspicious but curious. If this soldier really could make soup out of stones, no one would ever have to go hungry once they

knew the secret. The pot was produced, and the soldiers built a large fire in the middle of the town square.

They filled the pot with water, and soon the stones were cooking away in it. Pretty soon they attracted the attention of several people who stood around waiting to learn the secret of the soup.

One of the soldiers stirred the soup and tasted it. "Ah!" he said. "These are excellent stones. This would be the best soup we ever made if only it had a few vegetables."

"I have some carrots," said one villager.

"I have some turnips," said another.

"My mother has some beans," said a little girl.

Pretty soon everyone was running off and coming back with vegetables.

The soldier stirring the soup added the vegetables and tasted it again. "Wonderful," he exclaimed. "This will be the best soup ever. Only a little meat could make it better."

By this time more people had arrived and were getting into the spirit of things; they wanted to contribute something too.

"I have a little ham," said one.

"I have some bones," said another.

"I'll kill a chicken," said a third.

So quite a few people ran home and brought back some meat to put in the soup.

The soldier stirred some more and tasted the soup again. "It's almost ready," he said. "A little salt and pepper would make it perfect."

"I have that," said an old woman. "And some herbs; you should have those too."

Finally the soup was simmering away with the stones, vegetables, meat, salt and pepper, and herbs.

The soldier continued stirring the soup. "We'll need some bowls," he said.

By now the whole town was standing around, and all those who hadn't participated wanted to help so they could taste the soup and learn its secret. In a twinkling of an eye, bowls were produced and tables set up in the town square. People ran to their houses and looked into their cupboards to see what they could contribute. They returned with bread and butter, pies, cakes, and other dishes. Everything you would need for a feast was brought. Then the soldiers served the soup, and everyone agreed it was the best they had ever eaten.

The next morning all the townspeople turned out to say goodbye and to thank the soldiers again.

"Who would have guessed," they said, "that you could make such wonderful soup out of stones."

28

YOU CAN MAKE STONE SOUP

THIS RECIPE MAKES ENOUGH SOUP FOR THREE OR FOUR HUNGRY PEOPLE.

YOU NEED:

1 OR 2 CUPS OF CUT-UP, COOKED CHICKEN.

6 CUPS WATER

1 LARGE CHOPPED ONION

6 CHICKEN STOCK CUBES.

2 CUPS CHOPPED, RAW VEGETABLES (SUCH AS BEANS, CELERY, COURGETTES, CARROTS, CABBAGE, SPINACH, POTATOES)

A PINCH OF HERBS (PARSLEY, OREGANO, BASIL, THYME)

GET AN ADULT TO HELP WITH THIS PART.

1 CUP OF RAW RICE

PUT EVERYTHING INTO A LARGE PAN. PUT THE SOUP ON A HOT RING AND BRING IT TO THE BOIL. STIR IT VERY GENTLY. (IF YOU STIR TOO MUCH, THE CHICKEN MEAT WILL SHRED.) BOIL GENTLY FOR ABOUT 20 MINUTES, UNTIL THE VEGETABLES ARE TENDER AND THE RICE IS COOKED.

SERVE WITH BREAD AND BUTTER AND A GLASS OF MILK.

2
EXPEDITION TO AN OLD BOARD

There's a whole living world waiting to be discovered right under your feet! The animals of soil and leaves, which hide under boards and bricks, lead very interesting lives. Although these animals are common and easy to find, scientists are still learning new things about them. Some of them have hardly been studied at all.

Stop reading right now and go outside to dig up some of these creatures. Wait! First put a piece of damp paper towel in the bottom of a clean jar and take it with you. Soil animals need dampness to keep them alive while you watch them. Use a magnifying glass or hand lens. Some places to look are: under leaves, bricks, and boards; in the top layers of soil; and around the roots of plants.

Recyclers

Soil animals and plants are very important. They are the recyclers of our world. Imagine what would happen if dead things never decayed. Dead animals and plants would begin piling up, and pretty soon there would be no room for living things; and, even worse, there would be nothing left for them to live on. The important chemicals that living plants need in order to grow would be locked up in dead plants and animals. The recyclers keep this from happening by returning these chemicals to the soil.

30

EARTHWORM

EARWIG

CARABID BEETLE

NEWT

SPRINGTAIL WITH SPRING STRETCHED OUT

WITH SPRING BENEATH

CENTIPEDE

ROVE BEETLE

WOODLICE

MILLIPEDE

SNAIL

SOIL MITE

SLUG

Fungi

The "fungus among us" are not very conspicuous—and not fungus. *They* are "fungi," the word for more than one fungus. These important plants aren't green and can't make their own food. Soil fungi live on dead plants and animals and are important recyclers. They form white lacy patterns under leaves and rotting logs. Many fungi aren't seen because they're at work *inside* dead plants. (Some are at work inside live plants, but that's another story.)

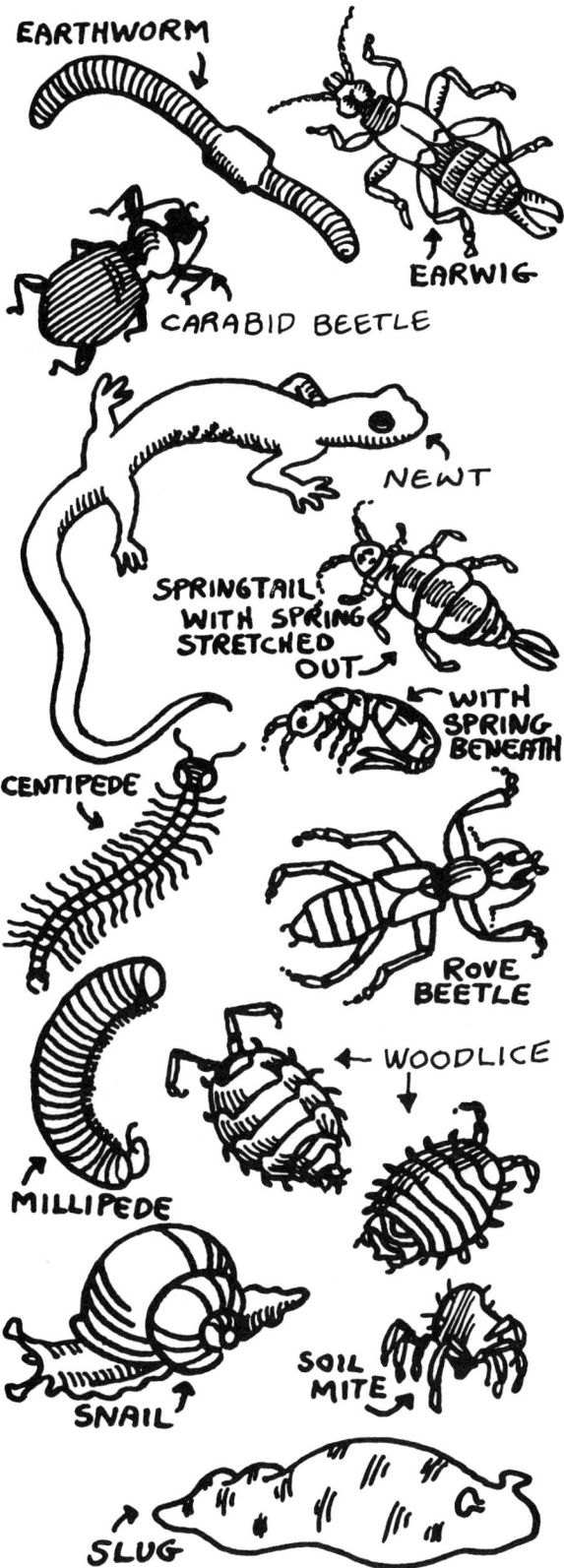

A FUNGUS GARDEN

YOU NEED A CLEAN JAR WITH A LID.

PUT A DAMP PAPER TOWEL IN THE BOTTOM OF THE JAR.

ADD SOMETHING FOR THE FUNGI TO GROW ON, SUCH AS BREAD, FRUIT, VEGETABLES, DEAD LEAVES. TRY ONE THING AT A TIME, OR USE DIFFERENT JARS FOR EACH ITEM.

The white lacy body of the fungus is called the "mycelium." When conditions are right, the fungus will make a fruiting body (one kind is a mushroom), which contains spores. Spores work the same way seeds do. Each spore can grow into a new fungus plant.

PUFFBALL

BREAD MOULD

The mushroom is a fruiting body everyone knows, but there are lots of other kinds. Some other fruiting bodies of recycling fungi are bracket fungi, bread mould, witches butter, and puffballs.

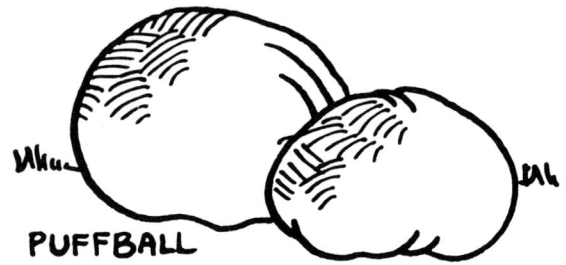

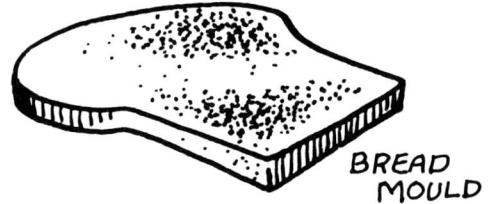

BRACKET FUNGI

WITCHES BUTTER

Spores are floating in the air around us. Fruits, vegetables, and dead leaves contain lots of spores, but fresh bread will have very few, unless you let it sit out of its wrapper for a few hours. Some bread is made with preservatives in it to keep it from getting mouldy. If you want to grow mould in your bread, use bread that has no preservatives.

Fungi need a moist environment, which is why you need a damp paper towel inside the jar and a lid. Put the jar in a dark place (some fungi grow best in the dark) and check it every day. When your fungus begins to grow, look at it with a hand lens or magnifying glass.

What Are You Growing?

Black mould on bread is probably the common bread

32

mould. Orange or reddish mould is most likely the red bread mould, *Neurospora*. Bluish green mould on fruit is usually *Penicillium*, a relative of the mould from which we get the medicine penicillin, which is used to treat some sicknesses caused by bacteria.

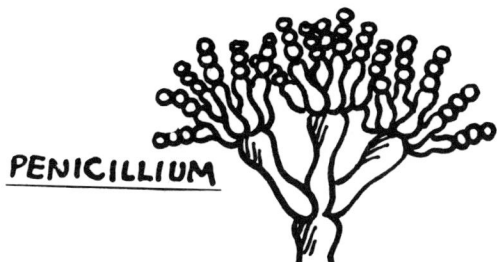

COMMON BREAD MOULD

<u>PENICILLIUM</u>

The common mushroom that is sold in supermarkets has brown spores, but wild mushrooms may have white, pink, yellow, brown, or black spores. If the spores are white, you can see them on white paper by looking across the surface of the paper. Use coloured paper to make a spore print. Ordinary mushrooms can shed 500,000 spores a minute for one or two days. Some kinds do even better at 80 million spores a minute for several days. You can see why the air around you is likely to have lots of spores in it.

HOW TO SEE A SPORE

ONE SPORE IS TOO TINY TO SEE BY ITSELF WITHOUT MAGNIFICATION, BUT THERE ARE TWO TRICKS THAT WILL LET YOU SEE SPORES WITHOUT MAGNIFICATION.

YOU CAN USE A WILD MUSHROOM OR ONE FROM THE SUPERMARKET. SPORES ARE FORMED ON THE GILLS, SO LOOK FOR A MUSHROOM THAT IS OLD ENOUGH TO HAVE GILLS SHOWING.

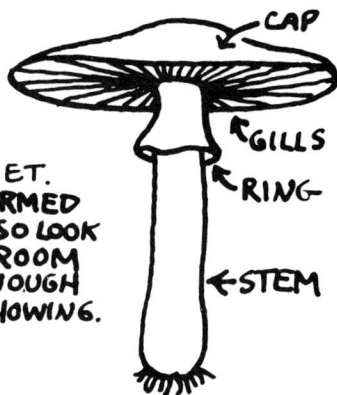

CAP

GILLS

RING

STEM

1. TAKE A MUSHROOM INTO A DARK ROOM AND SHINE A TORCH ON IT.

FALLING SPORES WILL REFLECT TINY DOTS OF LIGHT.

2. CUT THE STEM OFF THE CAP. SET THE CAP ON A PIECE OF PAPER.

COVER IT WITH A BOX OR A JAR. (THE COVER KEEPS OUT AIR CURRENTS AND LETS THE SPORES FALL DIRECTLY ONTO THE PAPER.) AFTER SEVERAL HOURS, YOU WILL HAVE A SPORE PRINT.

Why a Worm
Is Like a Plough

People who don't know any better speak of the lowly worm, but worms are extremely important to the health of soil. You can think of them as small but mighty ploughs, churning up the earth under our feet. Worms eat dead leaves and small pieces of plants that are mixed in with the soil. By pushing and eating their way through the soil, worms loosen it, making room for air and rain water to reach the roots of plants.

In addition to ploughing, worms also fertilize. Their droppings are rich food for plants.

When a plant grows, it takes in chemicals from the soil and builds them into leaves and stems. These chemicals are then locked up in the plant until something like a worm comes along. The worm eats dead leaves and digests them. The digestion process breaks down the chemicals. Some of the chemicals are used by the worm as food, and some pass out of the worm as droppings. The chemicals in worm droppings are ready for use again, this time by the plants.

It has been estimated that worms and other soil animals produce 105,000 pounds of dropping fertilizer per acre every year.

MANURE WORM

LARGE EARTHWORM

SMALL RED—BROWN WORMS

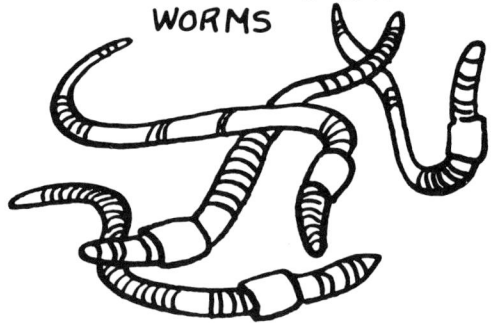

SMALL GREEN—BROWN WORMS

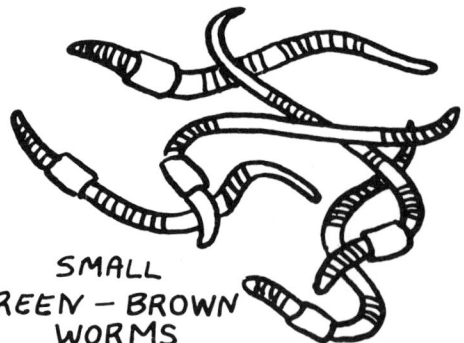

Making Life Easy for Worms

Some people breed worms to sell, and the places where worms are bred are called "worm farms." Red worms and manure worms are the kinds usually raised on farms. The farmer uses wooden boxes or concrete or brick beds to hold the worms. The bedding consists of plant material such as chopped hay, composted plants, peanut shells, or peat moss. Worms are fed manure (from cows, horses, or rabbits), compost, leaves, or even table scraps, if the farm is a small one. A good worm farm may have 35,000 worms per cubic metre!

Worms are sold for fish bait, to compost rabbit manure on rabbit farms, and as food in pet stores, zoos, and fish hatcheries.

Feeding Time at the Terrarium

Live and dead leaves, vegetable peels, and vegetable table scraps are good food for worms, springtails, woodlice, millipedes, and snails. These vegetarians can be kept happy for a long time in a small terrarium.

Centipedes, rove beetles, and carabid beetles are also predators. They will eat snails, worms, and small insects and, should be set free after a few days.

Give a Concert for Worms

Worms can't hear, but they are good at detecting vibrations. They can sense a person walking overhead or a mole digging through the soil.

Charles Darwin, the famous scientist, used to impress visitors with a simple demonstration of the earthworm's response to sound vibrations. He kept his worms in flowerpots on top of his piano. At night when the worms came out to eat leaves, Darwin would make them retreat into their burrows by playing low notes on the piano. He found that worms would duck back into

their burrows when he played some notes and not pay any attention to other notes.

You can try this yourself with a piano, guitar, banjo, violin, or other instrument that will support a jar with worms and soil in it. Set the jar right on top of the instrument. When the worms have come out by themselves (this will probably be in the evening when they come up for food), carefully perform your concert and watch the way your worms react.

Earwigs Are Good Mothers

Most female insects lay their eggs and leave them, but earwigs don't. An earwig mother takes care of her eggs. First she finds a good place to lay them. It might be in a hole or under a board or in some other protected spot. After the eggs are laid, the mother earwig guards them, moves them about, and licks them. If you find an earwig with eggs, you'll see that she usually

HOW TO MAKE A TERRARIUM

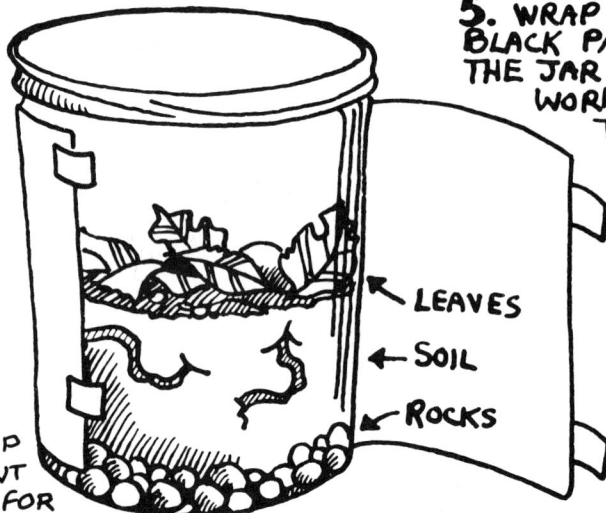

YOU NEED A LARGE JAR WITH A LID.

1. PUT AN INCH OF SMALL ROCKS IN THE BOTTOM FOR DRAINAGE.

2. ADD SEVERAL INCHES OF LOOSE SOIL.

3. COVER THE SOIL WITH DEAD LEAVES OR BARK.

4. SPRINKLE THE LEAVES REGULARLY WITH WATER TO KEEP THEM DAMP. (A PLANT SPRAYER IS IDEAL FOR THIS IF YOU HAVE ONE, OR MAKE YOUR OWN WITH AN OLD WINDOW-CLEANER BOTTLE. WASH IT AND RINSE THOROUGHLY TO CLEAN THE CHEMICALS OUT OF IT.)

← LEAVES
← SOIL
← ROCKS

5. WRAP A PIECE OF BLACK PAPER AROUND THE JAR SO THAT THE WORMS WILL MAKE THEIR TUNNELS AGAINST THE GLASS. THE ULTRAVIOLET PART OF SUNLIGHT IS DEADLY TO WORMS. ALTHOUGH ULTRAVIOLET LIGHT WON'T GO THROUGH MOST KINDS OF GLASS, THE WORMS DON'T KNOW THIS, SO THEY INSTINCTIVELY AVOID LIGHT.

has her body wrapped around them.

An earwig has a formidable weapon in her pincers, so be careful if you pick up one. Spiders and soft-bodied predatory insects such as rove beetles are even more vulnerable than your fingers are. Earwig pincers can stab right through their bodies. Earwigs use their pincers only to defend themselves.

Earwigs are leaf "skeletonizers." If you give an earwig plenty of fresh green leaves, you'll see that it prefers to eat the softer parts, ignoring the harder ones such as the veins and stems. When an earwig has finished with the leaf, all that's left is a skeleton.

Mother Woodlouse

Woodlice protect their eggs, but in a different way than earwigs do. The woodlouse mother lays her eggs in a special pouch formed by overlapping flaps under her abdomen. The pouch is called a "marsupium," which means pouch, or bag. Once woodlouse babies hatch, they leave the pouch and don't return. During summer and autumn many of the female woodlice you find will be carrying eggs.

Tracking Down Slugs and Snails

Early morning is the time to go out to hunt for slug and snail

ARE WOODLICE AFRAID OF THE DARK?

YOU CAN FIND OUT FOR YOURSELF. YOU NEED A SHOEBOX OR ANOTHER CARDBOARD BOX ABOUT THAT SIZE.

1. CUT A WINDOW IN ONE END OF THE TOP OF THE BOX.

2. PUT A PARTITION BETWEEN THE LIGHT AND DARK ENDS OF THE BOX, BUT LEAVE A CRAWL SPACE UNDER THE PARTITION SO THE WOODLICE CAN GET UNDER IT.

CRAWL SPACE

3. PUT SEVERAL WOODLICE IN EACH END OF THE BOX. COVER THE BOX AND WAIT A WHILE TO SEE WHAT HAPPENS.

4. REPEAT THIS EXPERIMENT WITH A DAMP PAPER TOWEL IN BOTH ENDS OF THE BOX. DOES THIS CHANGE THINGS?

OTHER THINGS TO TRY:

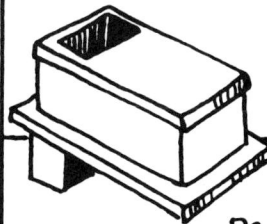

PUT THE BOX ON A TILTED SURFACE. DO THEY GO UP OR DOWN? DOES THE AMOUNT OF TILT CHANGE THE RESULTS?

DO THE ANIMALS PREFER A DAMP OR DRY SURFACE?

WHAT KINDS OF THINGS DO THEY LIKE TO EAT? (TRY RAW FRUITS AND VEGETABLES FROM YOUR REFRIGERATOR, AND LEAVES FROM YOUR GARDEN).

WHEN YOU ARE FINISHED WITH YOUR EXPERIMENTS, LET YOUR WOODLICE GO.

trails. Later the sun will have dried up those little patches of mucus, but until then you can easily see where the animals have been and what they've been up to. A slug or snail walks on one big foot, and its path is lubricated and smoothed by a layer of mucus, a slippery substance that comes out of glands just below the surface of the skin. Muscles in the animal's foot move it forward in waves.

Some kinds of snails can do a sort of march, moving one side of the foot at a time: left, right, left, right. This isn't a very fast way to travel, as you know if you've ever tried to walk with the laces of your two shoes tied together.

Sometimes gardeners use lime or ashes around their plants to protect them from snails. These substances burn the snail's tender foot. When the snail touches them, extra mucus comes out to protect the foot from the burning chemicals. Meanwhile the snail turns away to avoid this unpleasant feeling and leaves the garden.

Besides lubricating the trail, mucus helps to keep the snail's soft body from drying out. In dry weather the snail makes a door out of mucus to seal in moisture until the weather turns damp again.

To see snails and slugs in action, go outside with a torch

HAVE A SNAIL RACE

ALTHOUGH A SNAIL RACE ISN'T ESPECIALLY FAST, IT CAN BE FUN. EACH PERSON NEEDS:

A SNAIL

A PIECE OF NEWSPAPER

A FELT-TIP PEN

YOU ALSO NEED A CLOCK OR WATCH TO TIME THE RACE, AND A TAPE MEASURE TO MEASURE THE DISTANCE "RUN".

1. DAMPEN THE NEWSPAPERS SO THE SNAILS FEEL COMFORTABLE ON THEM.

2. EACH PERSON MARKS AN X IN THE CENTER OF HIS/HER PAPER AND PUTS THE SNAIL ON IT AT THE SIGNAL "GO".

3. AS THE SNAIL MOVES, DRAW ITS PATH WITH THE FELT-TIP PEN.

4. TIME THE RACE FOR 3 MINUTES, THEN CALL "STOP."

5. MEASURE HOW FAR EACH SNAIL HAS GONE. THE ANIMAL THAT "RAN" THE FARTHEST IS THE WINNER!

just after dark. Because these animals are in danger of drying out, they wait for damp dewy evenings or rainy days before wandering around.

Tip: To find snails, look under boards where there are weeds or garden plants. Snails also hide under leaves and inside clumps of plants. If your snail has sealed itself up during hot, dry weather, you can "wake it up" by dipping it in water for a few seconds.

Do Snails Eat Clover?

You can learn what snails like to eat by offering them different foods. Besides clover, try other plant leaves, both living and dead. Look for leaves with different textures. There are prickly leaves such as thistle, peppery leaves such as nasturtium, and furry leaves such as mullein.

Keep your snails in a clean jar with a damp paper towel. Holes should be punched in the lid with a nail and hammered flat so they don't cut you or the snails.

When you've finished your experiments, reward your snails by setting them free. Find a place away from the garden where there are plants for them to eat.

3
TREES ARE TERRIFIC

What good are trees? Maybe that's a silly question. Everybody can see what trees are good for. We build houses out of them, and boats. We use them for telephone poles. We make furniture and pencils. We grind them up to make paper. On cold days their wood warms us when we burn it in the fireplace or stove. Besides that, in the autumn you can rake their leaves together and jump in them. Trees are beautiful, and if you have one with large, strong branches, you can build a treehouse in it. Trees are obviously good neighbours to have, but they're much more than timber and telephone poles and warm fires on cold days.

Eat a Tree

Trees are food. Some produce food that humans can eat, such as apples, walnuts, and chestnuts. All trees make seeds, and those seeds are eaten. Maple, elm, willow, pine—small seeds and large are eaten by birds, squirrels, mice, and insects. More of a tree is eaten than just its seeds. Leaves, buds, twigs, bark, and even the wood can be eaten by one animal or another. Caterpillars eat leaves; squirrels and birds eat buds; wood-boring beetle larvae eat wood. The list goes on and on.

Home in a Tree

Trees are homes as well as food. Squirrels and birds build their nests in the branches. Insects live under the bark and inside leaves and twigs. Trees are like high-rise buildings with homes from the basement (roots) all the way to the penthouse (top branches).

Cool Breath

Trees provide shade on a hot summer day. But the shade of trees is cooler than the shade of an umbrella or a tall building. Trees are natural air conditioners! Every leaf has tiny openings called "stomata," and water evaporates from each "stoma" from the leaf. This

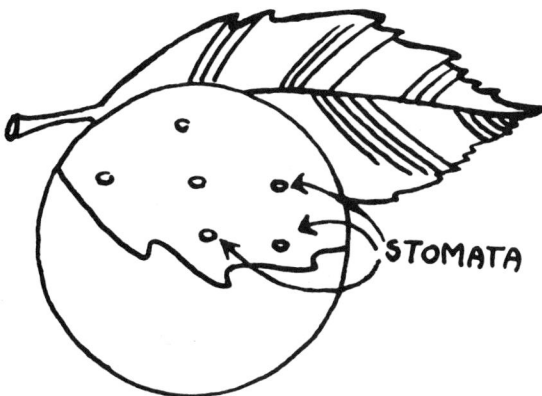

TRANSPIRATION

1. TIE A PLASTIC BAG AROUND SOME LEAVES.

2. CHECK THE BAG IN 1 TO 2 HOURS.

THE WATER YOU SEE WAS GIVEN OFF BY THE LEAVES IN A PROCESS CALLED "TRANSPIRATION."

process is called "transpiration". On a hot day a large tree will transpire litres of water. You can see this happening if you tie a plastic bag over some leaves. All plants transpire, but trees have so many leaves that they lose lots of water. Evaporation is how an air conditioner works. When water evaporates, it changes from being water to being a gas in the air. This change needs energy to make it happen, and the energy used up is heat. Hold a wet hand and a dry hand up in the air and see for yourself which gets cooler.

Pollution Removers

Trees are also antipollution devices. They catch smog. Smog particles in the air settle out and

STOMATA

stick to the leaves of trees. This helps clean the air and makes it better for us to breathe. Find some trees along a busy main road and see how dirty their leaves are. Compare them with tree leaves from a quiet street or from the country.

One of the most important things trees and all plants do is use up carbon dioxide and give off oxygen. The oxygen is used by animals, which include us. We breathe in the oxygen given off by plants and breathe out carbon dioxide, which the plants can use. This is the way plants and animals share the air around them. Each gives back what the other one needs and keeps those parts of the air in balance.

Adopt a Tree

Everyone should have his or her own personal tree. It doesn't have to be on your property as long as you can visit it whenever you like. A tree is a nice friend to have. It listens to what you have to say. It doesn't yell or talk back or tell you what to do. It doesn't ask where you've been when you haven't visited it for a while. And it's always there when you need someone to listen. So find a tree you like and give it a big hug. Then sit down under its branches and get acquainted.

Listen to the Trees Talking

Not everybody knows this, but trees do talk. Some trees talk almost all the time, and others talk only once in a while. Some are loud and clattery; others are quiet and whispery. When the air is still, they hardly say anything at all, but when the wind blows hard, they sigh and shout. Some trees even sing.

Listen to different trees. Pine trees sound different from poplars. Oak trees sound different from willows. Dry leaves make a crackling rustle in the autumn, and empty branches blown by winter winds have a sound all their own. Most people never hear trees talk because they don't take the time to listen. If you want to hear trees talk, or bees buzz, or any other special sound, all you have to do is listen.

What Can You Say to a Tree?

People might think you are just a bit strange if you stand on the street corner chatting away to your tree, But there is a way to talk, not just to your tree, but also to yourself. You do it by keeping a diary, where you write what you want. You can write things about your tree: what it looks like, how it sounds. You can trace a leaf or note the day it starts to bloom or when it changes colour in the autumn. You can describe your tree's residents and visitors—the insects, birds, and squirrels you see. By keeping a record you can learn a a lot about when things happen to your tree. You can also write down the things you think about when you sit under your tree—things you might not want to tell just anybody, except a good solid friend who won't tell anyone else.

Pressing Leaves

There are lots of ways to get to know your tree. You can study its leaves, examine its flowers, and collect and plant its seeds. You can watch the animals that live in and on it, and soon you'll learn the secret of how to tell whether an animal has been there.

It's easy to make a leaf record of your tree and its friends. Tree leaves are usually dry enough to press in a book without damaging the pages. If you aren't sure about this, however, put the leaves between two sheets of newspaper before you put them in the book.

You Can Press Flowers and Greens

Flowers, grasses, and other plants are usually too wet to put in books. You can make a small press for them with cardboard from a grocery box, newspaper, and rubber bands. Press

HOW TO PRESS FLOWERS AND GREENS

YOU CAN MAKE A SMALL PRESS USING CARDBOARD FROM GROCERY BOXES, NEWSPAPER, AND RUBBER BANDS.

CARDBOARD
NEWSPAPER
LEAF

A RUBBER BAND WILL HOLD IT ALL TIGHTLY TOGETHER.

PRESS LEAVES SEVERAL DAYS TO A WEEK, UNTIL THEY ARE DRY.

HOW TO MAKE LEAF PICTURES

1. PLACE SOME PRESSED LEAVES BETWEEN TWO SHEETS OF WAXED PAPER.

2. PUT THE WAXED PAPER BETWEEN TWO SHEETS OF NEWSPAPER.

3. IRON OVER THE NEWSPAPER. SET THE IRON AT "MEDIUM" OR "WOOL."

4. EVEN THE EDGES OF YOUR PICTURE WITH SCISSORS, OR CUT A DESIGN AROUND THE LEAVES.

5. MAKE A HOLE IN ONE END AND TIE WOOL OR STRING THROUGH IT. HANG IT UP!

the leaves for several days or a week, until they're dry.

Making Pictures with Leaves

You can glue or tape your pressed leaves into a scrapbook, or glue them onto note paper and use it to write a letter to a friend. Dried leaves can be ironed between pieces of waxed paper and hung in the window for decoration.

If you can't find the right ink, buy a stamp pad (the kind for rubber stamps) at a hardware shop or in a stationery shop. Sometimes even supermarkets have them. Rub the underside of your leaf on the pad. Lay it ink side down on the paper and press once.

The Well-dressed Tree

Like people, different trees dress differently. Not only do they have different leaves, their bark is different too. The next time you walk down a street with trees on it, see how many different kinds of bark you can find. Some bark is knobby and broken, some makes long curving lines up the trunk, and some is smooth. Sycamore, London plane, and some other trees shed their bark. It peels off in patches or strips to expose new bark underneath. Bark is very important to trees. It protects them

PRINT WITH PLANTS

MATERIALS;
WATER-BASED INK
A FLAT, STIFF BRUSH
NEWSPAPER
SOFT PAPER (LIKE RICE PAPER)

1. PRESS A LEAF FOR A FEW MINUTES TO FLATTEN IT. (IF IT GETS TOO DRY, THE VEINS WON'T SHOW, SO DON'T WAIT TOO LONG.)

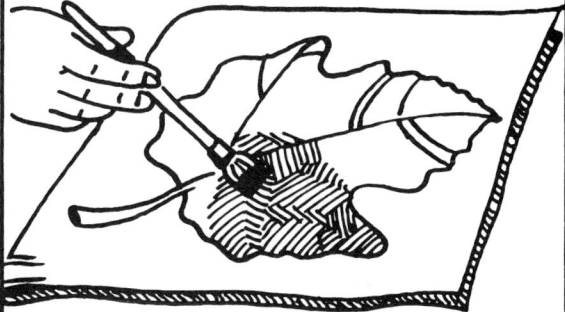

2. LAY THE LEAF UPSIDE DOWN ON NEWSPAPER AND PAINT IT WITH INK. NOTICE THAT YOU PAINT THE UNDERSIDE OF THE LEAF.

3. TRANSFER LEAF TO CLEAN NEWSPAPER, INK SIDE UP.

4. LAY THE SOFT PAPER OVER THE LEAF CAREFULLY.

5. PRESS ONCE ONLY. HOLD LEAF AT THE STEM AND RUN YOUR FINGERS OUT TO THE TIP.

THAT'S IT!

YOU CAN USUALLY GET SEVERAL PRESSINGS FROM ONE INKING. ALTHOUGH THE FIRST PRINTING IS DARKEST, SOMETIMES THE LIGHTER ONES LOOK BETTER.

HOW TO MAKE PLANT PAPERS

YOU WILL NEED:
HEAVY PAPER
TISSUE
PVA GLUE
A PAINT BRUSH

1. LAY A PRESSED LEAF ON HEAVY PAPER AND COVER IT WITH ONE LAYER OF TISSUE.

2. DILUTE SOME PVA GLUE WITH WATER. USE ABOUT HALF GLUE AND HALF WATER.

3. DAB GLUE ONTO TISSUE WITH BRUSH. (IT'S SUPPOSED TO GET WRINKLED.) WHEN THE TISSUE IS ALL WET, STOP AND LET IT DRY.
PLANT PAPERS MAKE NICE GREETING CARDS.

from injury and invasion by insects and disease.

Just under the tough outer bark are layers of growing and water-carrying cells. All the water going up to the leaves and the nutrients going down to the roots are carried in these layers. Taking the bark off usually destroys these important layers of cells. When the leaves can't get water and the roots can't get food, the tree dies.

Rub a Tree

You can study bark without taking it off the tree by making bark rubbings.

BARK RUBBING

1. HOLD A PIECE OF PAPER AGAINST THE TREE.

2. RUB A CRAYON OVER THE PAPER UNTIL THE BARK PATTERN SHOWS.

SOME BARK NEEDS A VERY LIGHT PRESSURE TO MAKE A GOOD RUBBING. OTHER BARK NEEDS A FIRMER HAND. YOU'LL HAVE TO EXPERIMENT TO FIND OUT WHICH IS BEST FOR EACH TREE.

MAGNOLIA
BLOSSOMS

Flowers in the Air

Spring is the time when trees flower. Apples, plums and other fruit trees, magnolias and haw-thorns—all have bright flowers with a sweet smell. The colour and smell of these flowers attract insects. Bees, flies, beetles, butterflies, and moths travel from flower to flower, drinking nectar or gathering pollen. Flower pollen sticks to an insect's body, then when the insect visits another flower, some of the pollen sticks to that flower's seed-producing part, its "stigma." Insects get food from flowers, and flowers receive pollen so they can grow seeds. Although some flowers can self-pollinate, the seeds that form when a tree is pollinated by another tree of the same kind grow into healthier trees. This process is called "cross-pollina-tion." It took millions of years for plants and insects to develop this way of helping each other.

Air Transportation

Have you ever seen the flowers of oak trees? They are small, greenish, and don't have any smell. Insects don't need to find them because they are wind pollinated. The wind carries pollen from one tree to another. Some of our commonest plants are wind pollinated, grasses and plantains to name two.

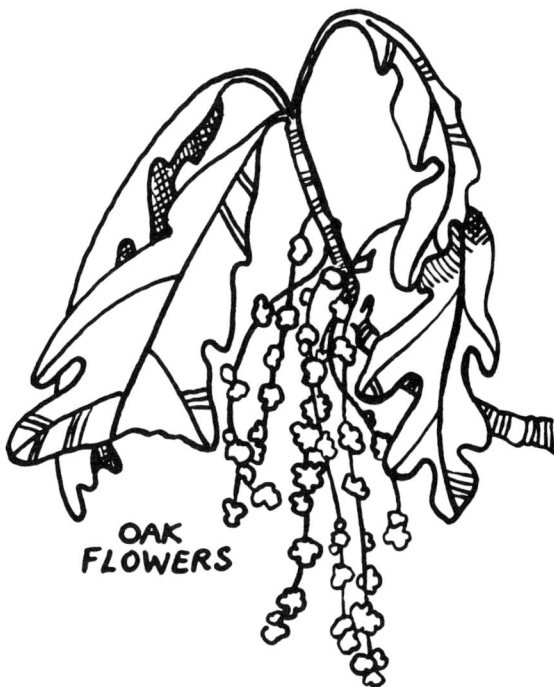

OAK
FLOWERS

47

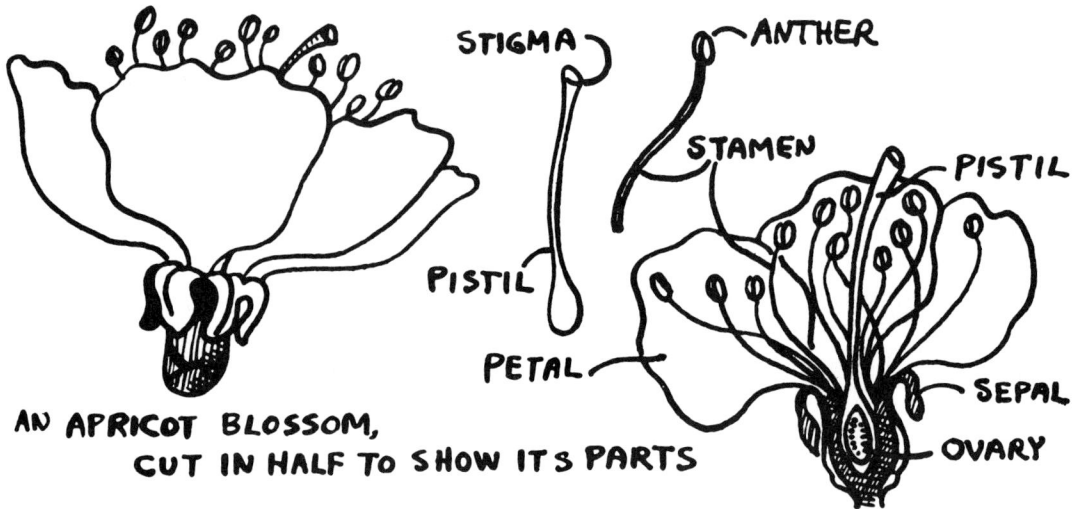

STIGMA · ANTHER · STAMEN · PISTIL · PISTIL · PETAL · SEPAL · OVARY

AN APRICOT BLOSSOM, CUT IN HALF TO SHOW ITS PARTS

Wind-pollinated flowers produce lots of pollen, a necessity because the wind blows every which way and much of the pollen is wasted. Insect-pollinated flowers make less pollen and put some of their energy into bright flowers and nectar, both of which attract the insects. They need less pollen because insects deliver it for them.

Help the Flowers

You can be a pollinator too. Tree flowers are hard to reach, so look for other kinds. Brush the anthers (see drawing) gently with your finger or a piece of cotton. Pollen looks like dust and is usually yellow or orange. Take it to the stigma of another flower and rub it off gently onto the sticky surface. You may have to try several flowers before you find pollen. Some will have already released their pollen, and others won't be ready yet. Watch bees for a clue. When scientists want to grow new or special varieties of plants, they pollinate the plants in just this way. Then they cover the flowers with plastic or paper so that no other pollen can reach them.

HAWTHORN

Travelling Seeds

Trees can really get around. Some of them run on four legs, some fly with wings, and others soar high into the air because they are light and fluffy. Of course, trees do not do all this when they're old and tall and have their roots firmly in the ground. They travel when they are young, as seeds.

Some tree seeds are born to glide. They have thin wings, which stick out on one side or all around. When the wind blows, they are whirled away, spinning like helicopters or floating like saucers. Sycamores, elms, pines, spruces, and many other trees have soaring seeds. See how far you can get them to go by gathering them up and throwing them into the wind on a breezy day.

Some trees, such as willows and poplars, can fly even farther. The seeds of these trees are very tiny and light. Each one is equipped with a parachute of fine hairs. Even a gentle breeze can lift these seeds high over the treetops and carry them many miles to a new place.

ELM

SPRUCE

PINE

SYCAMORE

WOOLLY WILLOW SEEDS

Borrowed Wings

Some seeds that fly don't have their own wings at all. They travel many miles through the air safe in the stomach of a bird. Cherry, raspberry, and other large fruits usually get to new places this way. A bird eats the sweet fruit and swallows the seed inside at the same time.

49

The bird digests the soft parts of the fruit, but the seed is protected by a hard shell. It passes through the bird's digestive tract and gets deposited in a new place to grow. Seeds that travel inside birds get a head start in life. Not only do they get a free ride, they are dropped with a dab of ready-made fertilizer. Seeds pass through people too. The fertilizer sludge from a sewage treatment plant is full of tomato seeds all ready to sprout.

Seeds That Move on Four Legs

Many seeds are too heavy to fly and too big to swallow whole. These are the ones that travel on four legs. Acorns, walnuts, chestnuts, and other large, heavy seeds get to new places by being carried by squirrels, voles, mice and other rodents. Many are eaten, of course, but others are buried in specially dug holes or stored in burrows and forgotten. Those that aren't eaten will sprout, and their strong shoots can push their way out of an inch or more of earth.

Tree Detective

Often things happen in nature that you can't see, but if you're a good detective, you can figure out what's been going on. The

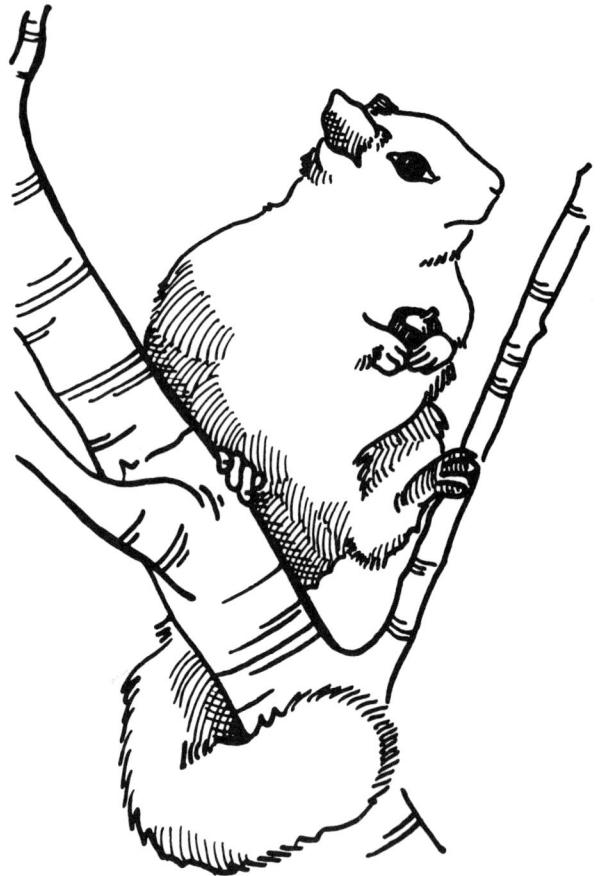

50

DO ROOTS ALWAYS GROW DOWN?

YOU CAN ANSWER THIS QUESTION FOR YOURSELF, AND START SOME TREES GROWING AT THE SAME TIME.

1. GATHER SOME SYCAMORE, ELM, OR OTHER TREE SEEDS. SOME MAY NOT SPROUT, SO USE SEVERAL.

2. SOAK THE SEEDS IN WATER FOR 3 TO 4 HOURS.

3. PUT THE SEEDS BETWEEN WET NEWSPAPERS OR PAPER TOWELS. KEEP THE PAPER WET AND LOOK AT THE SEEDS EVERY DAY.

4. WHEN THE ROOTS BEGIN TO PUSH OUT, WATCH WHICH WAY THEY GROW. TRY TURNING THE SEEDS OVER TO SEE IF YOU CAN CHANGE THEIR DIRECTION.

5. WHEN THE FIRST LEAVES PUSH THEIR WAY OUT OF THE SEED, YOU CAN WATCH THEM TOO.

THE TENDENCY TO GROW DOWN IS CALLED "GEOTROPISM."

THE TENDENCY TO GROW TOWARD THE LIGHT IS CALLED "PHOTOTROPISM."

6. WHEN YOUR SEEDS HAVE SPROUTED, PLANT THEM OUTSIDE. LOOK FOR SPOTS THAT HAVE ROOM FOR TREES. IF YOU PLANT YOUR SEEDS AT THE SAME TIME THEY WOULD BEGIN TO GROW NATURALLY, THEY PROBABLY WON'T NEED ANY SPECIAL CARE. IF YOU PLANT THEM AT SOME OTHER TIME, THEY MAY NEED TO BE WATERED OR PROTECTED FROM COLD UNTIL THEY'RE OLDER AND LARGER.

most important thing you can do is to pay attention.

Find a hole in the trunk or branches of a tree. Ask yourself, "Is the hole big, medium-size, or little? Does it go into the tree or can I see the end of it? Is the tree partly dead and hollow? Is the trunk large enough to shelter a woodpecker or squirrel?"

Small holes were probably made by insects. Wood-boring beetle larvae live under bark and inside tree trunks. When they become adult beetles, they bore their way out and leave behind small holes.

Small holes that create a pattern on the tree trunk may have been made by woodpeckers. These birds peck off small pieces of bark when searching for adult insects and grubs to eat.

Medium-size holes are probably bird holes. Woodpeckers make holes for nests. They may use the same holes year after year. When the woodpeckers leave, other birds and squirrels may use their holes.

HOW TO MAKE A ROOTARIUM

YOU CAN USE ANY SEEDS FOR THIS. TREE SEEDS ARE GREAT, BUT IF YOU DON'T HAPPEN TO HAVE ANY HANDY, DRIED BEANS FROM THE SUPERMARKET WORK TOO.

1. SOAK THE SEEDS IN WATER FOR 3 TO 4 HOURS.

2. WET SOME PAPER TOWELS AND LINE A CLEAR GLASS JAR WITH THEM. STUFF THE CENTRE OF THE JAR WITH DRY PAPER OR FOIL TO KEEP THE WET TOWELS AGAINST THE SIDES.

3. PLANT YOUR SEEDS BETWEEN THE TOWELS AND THE JAR SIDES, WHERE YOU CAN SEE THEM.

4. KEEP THE TOWELS WET. WHEN YOUR SEEDS SPROUT, YOU CAN WATCH THE ROOTS THROUGH THE GLASS.

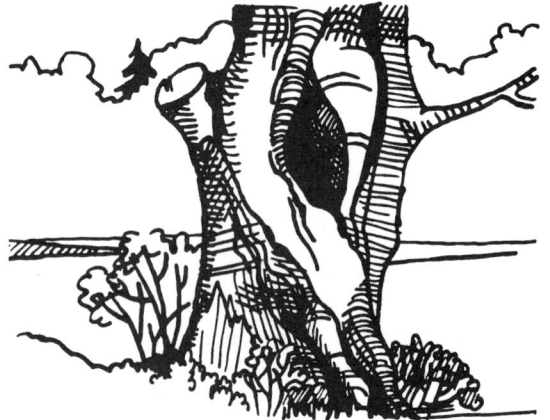

Large holes in hollow trees may be used by larger birds such as tawny owls or by squirrels. If there's mud or soft soil near the tree, look for the tracks of these animals.

How to Find Nests

Your eyes and ears can help you locate nests, both in holes and in tree branches. Watch for birds picking up twigs or string in the spring. If you are patient, you may see them carry this nesting material to the home they are building. Later in the spring, birds will be gathering insects and worms to carry to their chicks. They sometimes take detours when returning to a nest of chicks (to protect their chicks) and may fly to other trees or branches on their way home, so it's very challenging to follow them. When the parent returns with food, all the chicks cry to show how hungry they are, so listen for peeping baby birds.

Does a Bird Perch Here?

Birds are creatures of habit just as people are. Do you usually sit at the same place at the table? Birds do this too. At night a bird will usually sit on the same branch. Flycatchers, hawks, and owls often sit in the same place when they are between hunting flights. You can find these perches by watching for groups of bird droppings. Owl perches usually have collections of owl pellets under them. The pellets contain bones and hair from the owl's prey. You can tell what an owl has been eating by taking apart a pellet.

Are there actually owls in cities? You bet there are! Most people never see them because they fly at dusk or later and sleep during the day. City owls hunt over parks, fields, and other open areas. They roost in trees, empty buildings, and church towers.

53

Christmas Trees

Most of us can't imagine Christmas without a tree. And yet if you think about it, cutting down a tree, bringing it into our home, and hanging things on the branches might seem a little strange to someone who hasn't grown up with that custom. The first Christmas trees were cut in Germany, and the idea spread from there to other countries. German people brought the custom of cutting and decorat-ing Christmas trees to Britain in the reign of Queen Victoria. In those days there were trees all around and far fewer people. It was easy to go out to the woods near your house and cut an evergreen tree just the right size for a Christmas tree. Today there are fewer trees, and most people live a long way from the woods, which are now someone's private property. Although Christmas trees can still be cut by permit in some forests, most trees we decorate are grown on Christmas tree farms or in nurseries.

Tree Farms

A tree farm has many advantages over the wild woods. When trees are cut in a natural forest, people often don't replace them by planting new ones. Long ago this didn't matter because there were more trees and fewer people. Today with millions of people wanting Christmas trees, cutting without replanting would mean that there wouldn't be enough small trees for future Christmases. On a tree farm new trees are planted every year to replace cut ones. These trees are spaced so that they all have a chance to grow evenly. They're often carefully pruned to improve their natural shape. Each year a certain number have grown to just the right size for cutting.

Living Trees

Nurseries sell live trees all year round, but at Christmas they often have potted trees, which are large enough to decorate. A live tree doesn't dry out and drop its needles. After Christmas it can be planted in your garden or given to a park. You can also leave the tree in its pot and put it outside until next Christmas. A live tree, properly cared for, can celebrate many Christmases with you.

Cut-Tree Care

A cut tree will stay green and keep its needles longer if you keep it outside, protected from sun and wind until just before Christmas. If you live where a bucket of water won't freeze, put the tree in water. Cut an inch or so off the bottom of the trunk first. If it's cold enough that water freezes outdoors where you live, wait until you bring the tree inside to put it in water.

Water evaporates quickly in a heated house, so check the bucket every day and add water when necessary.

When it's time to take down the tree, you can cut off a few branches and put them in water. The branches will stay green for as long as several months and may even grow roots. If you want to encourage the branches to root, buy a root hormone from a nursery and add it to the water. When your branches grow roots, you can plant them outside.

Caring for a Live Tree

The soil where your tree is growing should be kept damp but not soggy. Soil fungi can cause tree roots to rot if they are too wet. Put a sheet of plastic or a bucket under your tree to keep the rug and floor dry. It's best to put the tree near a window or other cool place and not near a heater or radiator.

Your live tree won't be hurt if it doesn't get much light for a week or so, but after Christmas, move it outside where it can get some sun.

Outdoors a potted tree will still need to be watered. The soil should nearly (but not quite) dry out between waterings.

If the tree grows very fast, you may need to prune it a little. Eventually it will need a larger pot.

4
ANTS IN THE FLOWERPOT

Ants are very close neighbours. They live in the ground around and under our houses. Sometimes they even come inside. They invade our kitchens for food. When the weather is dry, they come in for water; and when the weather is wet, they come in to escape the water-logged soil outside. During a heavy rain, ants may take up residence in the dry soil under and around the house. From there it's an easy climb into a tasty kitchen. Once inside the house, ants may even move into the flowerpots to set up house-keeping. A flowerpot provides a nice home: the weather is good, the air is warm, and the kitchen is nearby.

Make the Best of an Ant Invasion

Unfortunately, what is convenient for ants isn't always convenient for people. Not every-one likes ants with their peanut butter and jam sandwiches, for example, but there are some things you can do to make living with ants a little easier.

First of all you can keep them out of your kitchen and any other place you don't want them by using insect repellent. Get a can of spray insect repellent (the kind that's safe to spray on your skin). Spray a line of repellent around the doors, windows, and walls where the ants come into the room. Ants don't like the repellent and won't cross it. You'll have to respray the line every three to four days as the effect wears off.

Now if you don't mind the ants in your flowerpots, you can help keep them happy (and out of the rest of the house) by feeding them. Crumbled, dog or cat biscuits, cake crumbs, meat scraps, and sweet things are some of the foods ants like. Some ants are more attracted to sweet food, while others like meat.

Ants in the house are handy subjects for the experiments described in this chapter. If you don't want them running around loose, build an ant farm for them.

Kinds of Ants

An ant is an ant is an ant. All ants look so much alike that it's unlikely you'd mistake one for anything else. Even though ants look alike, there are many different kinds. And there are some animals that are ant mimics; they look like ants but aren't.

The basic ant plan is very useful, and this is probably why so many kinds of ants look alike. Without changing their shape, ants have been able to move into different habitats and use different kinds of food. Here is a sample of ant types and lifestyles.

Carpenter ants live in dead trees and rotting logs in many parts of the world. They make extensive tunnels through the wood. Sometimes they move into houses and live in walls, doors, wooden steps, or wherever there is wood. Carpenter ants eat small insects.

Twig ants live inside plant stems, thorns, acorns, and galls. They are found mostly in places such as South America, Africa, and the United States. Twig dwellers cut holes in twigs that have soft centres and hollow out the inside. Signs are round holes in white ash and sumach trees. Some of these ants eat honeydew, which they collect from aphids.

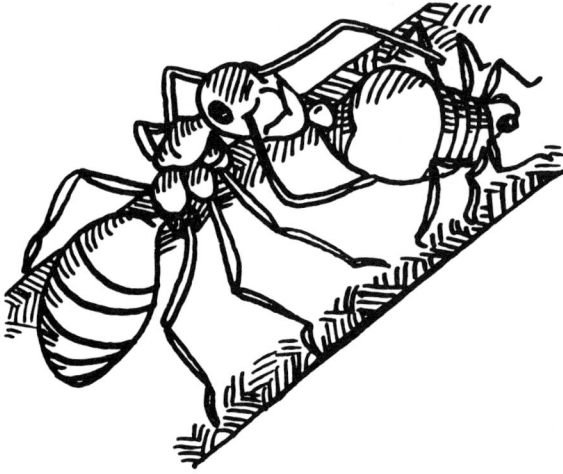

Mushroom farmers live underground where they grow fungus gardens. Some of these ants gather small pieces of plants to use as compost for their fungus beds. Other mushroom farmers called "leaf-cutting ants" cut up leaves and flower petals and carry them home for compost. Leaf cutters live mainly in the tropics.

inside the abdomens of ants called "repletes." A full replete has an abdomen the size of a grape and is so heavy that it can't move around by itself. A replete hangs from the roof of an underground room and is filled when honeydew is available and is emptied by the other ants when it's not. When an ant is hungry, it goes to a replete and taps it with its antenna. This signals the replete to spit out a drop of honeydew for the hungry ant. Honeypot ants live in dry areas like Australia and the south west of the United States. Few people have ever seen a live replete because they stay in burrows several feet underground.

Honeypot ants collect honeydew, which is secreted by aphids. They store the honeydew

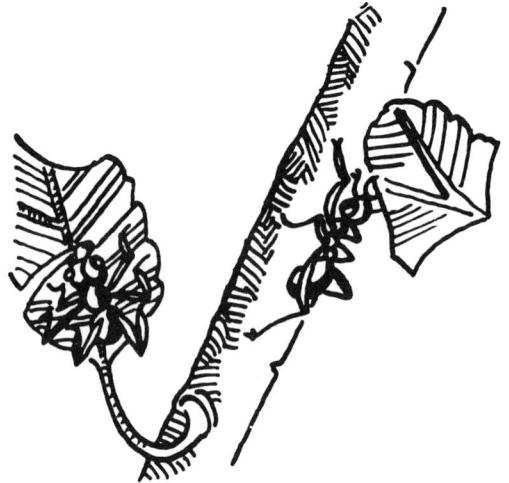

Aphid herders tend aphids, which are sometimes called "ant cows." Aphids are small insects that suck plant juices and produce weak sugar water

MAKE AN ANT FARM

YOU NEED:
A LARGE JAR   TAPE
PLASTER OF PARIS   A HAMMER
THIN CARDBOARD   A THIN NAIL
A PIECE OF SPONGE   A CLEAN TIN.
      SOME BLACK PAPER

1. MAKE A CYLINDER OF CARDBOARD THAT WILL FIT DOWN INSIDE THE JAR. LEAVE ABOUT 2.5 cm BETWEEN IT AND THE SIDES OF THE JAR.

2. FASTEN THE CYLINDER WITH TAPE.

3. MIX A BATCH OF PLASTER OF PARIS IN THE CLEAN TIN. PUT THE WATER IN FIRST, THEN ADD PLASTER. THE MIXTURE SHOULD BE ALMOST AS THICK AS SOFT WHIPPING CREAM.

4. POUR THE PLASTER INTO THE CENTRE OF THE CARDBOARD INSIDE THE JAR UNTIL IT'S 3/4 FULL.

5. LET THE PLASTER SET UNTIL HARD, ABOUT 1 TO 2 HOURS. THEN CUT OFF THE EXTRA CARDBOARD WITH A KNIFE.

6. USING THE NAIL, PUNCH TINY HOLES, SMALLER THAN YOUR ANTS, IN JAR LID.

7. PUT A SMALL PIECE OF WET SPONGE ON THE PLASTER FOR MOISTURE. KEEP THE SPONGE WET.

8. TAPE BLACK PAPER OVER THE OUTSIDE OF THE JAR SO THE ANTS WILL MAKE THEIR NEW TUNNELS AGAINST THE GLASS.

from this plant sap. Many ants visit aphids for this sweet honeydew. Some actually herd the aphids around, protecting them, carrying them to fresh plants, and tending their eggs in underground burrows. Watch for ants running up the stems of plants or trees, and then look to see if they're tending aphids. You may get to see one "milk" its "cow" by tapping it with its antennae.

Harvester ants build large ant-hills with the soil dug from their burrows. They harvest seeds, which they store in special underground store-rooms.

9. NOW YOU ARE READY TO COLLECT ANTS AND PUT THEM, ALONG WITH THEIR SOIL, INTO YOUR ANT FARM. THE SOIL SHOULD BE LOOSELY DROPPED INTO THE SPACE BETWEEN THE PLASTER AND THE GLASS.

10. FEED YOUR ANTS SUGAR WATER, BITS OF DRY DOG FOOD, AND TABLE SCRAPS. BY TRYING DIFFERENT KINDS OF FOOD, YOU'LL SOON LEARN WHAT THEY PREFER.

Ants for Your Farm

Ants are everywhere: on plants, under stones, on the trees, along pavements, inside houses. The ant farm is for small ground-nesting ants. Look for lines of ants marching along pavements or paths and follow the columns back to the nest. Dig up the nest carefully and try to get as many ants as you can. The queen is the most important one to capture if you want your colony to continue living in the farm for a long time.

Another way to get an ant colony is to find one that has moved into a flowerpot. Sometimes you can encourage a colony to do this by filling a flowerpot with soil and putting it outdoors on top of an ant-hill. Water the ground so the ant-hill gets thoroughly soaked. This will cause the ants to move to dryer ground, hopefully right into your flowerpot.

Trail Tricks with Ants

Some ants find their way by sight, some follow scent trails laid down by other ants from the colony, and some do a little of each. There's a way to find out if ants are following a scent trail.

Feeding Ants

Gather different kinds of food from around your house to take

TRAIL TRICK ONE

YOU NEED:
PAPER
A PENCIL
TAPE

1. FIND A TRAIL OF ANTS ALONG A PAVEMENT OR OTHER FLAT SURFACE.

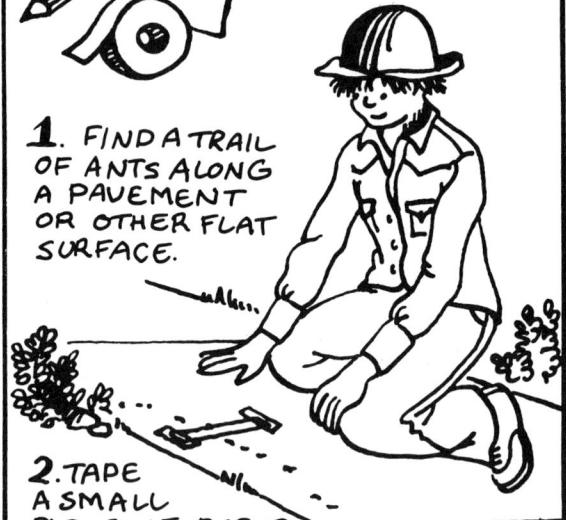

2. TAPE A SMALL PIECE OF PAPER (ABOUT 2.5 cm WIDE) OVER PART OF THE TRAIL.

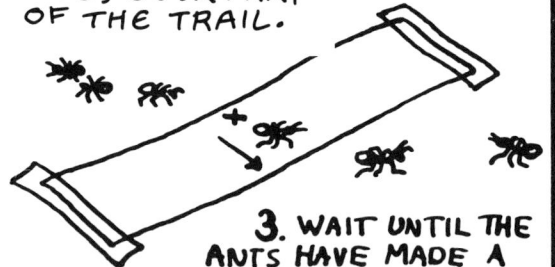

3. WAIT UNTIL THE ANTS HAVE MADE A NEW TRAIL ACROSS THE PAPER. MARK THE START OF THE NEW TRAIL WITH AN X AND DRAW AN ARROW FOR ITS DIRECTION.

4. KEEPING X AT THE SAME PLACE, TURN THE PAPER.

SEE IF THE ANTS FOLLOW THE PATH ON THE PAPER, OR CONTINUE IN THE RIGHT DIRECTION. IF THEY FOLLOW THE PAPER PATH, THEY ARE ORIENTING TO SCENT ON PAPER.

outside to an ant trail. Offer them one at a time to the ants. Watch as the first ant finds the food, then watch what the ant does. Ants can't talk, but they do convey excitement to other ants with the speed and frequency of their antennae taps and with scent. Which food do the ants get most excited about? If the pieces of food are too big for one ant to carry but small enough for several ants to move, you may get to see some teamwork. How ants decide to team up is a mystery. Ants are fascinating to watch, and we still have a great deal to learn about them.

TRAIL TRICK TWO

LOOK FOR AN ANT TRAIL ON THE SOIL. FIRST, PICK UP LARGE STONES, LEAVES, AND OTHER VISUAL CLUES THE ANTS MIGHT BE USING TO FIND THEIR WAY. DON'T DISTURB THE GROUND RIGHT UNDER THE TRAIL IN CASE THERE'S SCENT ON IT.

IF YOUR ANTS BECOME CONFUSED WHEN THE VISUAL PARTS OF THE TRAIL ARE REMOVED, YOU KNOW THAT VISION PLAYS A PART IN THEIR TRAILS.

5
MICE AND RATS

Rats have followed people all over the world. Both the black rat and brown rat originated in Asia. Hundreds of years ago when people lived in small tribes and didn't travel long distances, these rats didn't travel much either. As people began to travel, the rats travelled with them as stowaways in boxes and bags of grain and food. Some went by caravan and others by ship. Today rats live almost everywhere that people do.

Since people live nearly everywhere on the earth and rats do too, you might expect to find that people and rats have some things in common. You're absolutely right! People and rats are very adaptable. They can eat a wide variety of food; they can live in a wide variety of places; they can adapt to different conditions; they learn fast.

Rats, Upstairs and Down

Although black and brown rats are similar, they do have different preferences. Brown rats like living on the ground, and those that live in houses usually live downstairs or in the basement. They don't mind the damp and will set up housekeeping in sewers and on river banks. Rubbish dumps and waste lands are often full of brown rat burrows.

Black rats were mostly driven

out of their home areas by the brown rats when they came to Britain from Russia in the 18th century. They mostly live in seaports now.

Rats Are Clever

Rats have been taught to run mazes, push buttons to have their food delivered, and avoid things that give them a shock. Since rats learn quickly and are easy to keep in a laboratory, they make ideal subjects for studying how animals learn. Psychologists and psychology students have been observing the way rats learn for many years, and whole books have been written about it. These studies are quite fascinating and very useful. Many of our studies of human behaviour and learning began with something that was learned about rats.

The life of a rat may depend on how clever it is. Rats are suspicious of traps and hard to catch. They often learn to avoid poisoned bait, and once one rat avoids a certain bait, all the other rats associated with it do the same.

Rats are suspicious of new things, so give yours time to get used to the maze. Repeat the experiment several times, letting your rat eat a little of the food each time. Clever rats will

MAKE A MAZE FOR RATS

YOU NEED: SCISSORS
               MASKING TAPE
5 EMPTY LARGE MILK CARTONS
     PEANUT BUTTER OR RAISINS
   A WATCH WITH A SECOND HAND
          A PET RAT

MAKE A T-SHAPED MAZE.

1. CUT BOTH ENDS OFF THREE CARTONS.

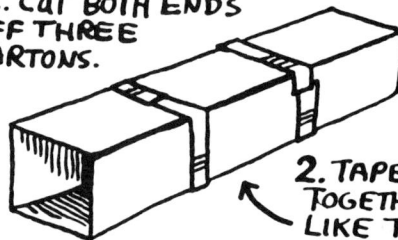

2. TAPE THEM TOGETHER LIKE THIS.

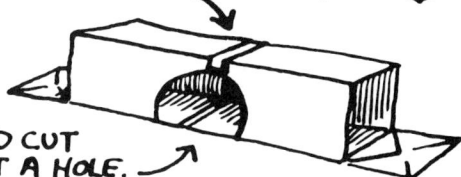

3. CUT THE POURING ENDS OFF TWO MILK CARTONS, THEN CUT THE BOTTOMS LOOSE, LEAVING THEM ATTACHED ON ONE SIDE LIKE THIS.

4. TAPE THEM TOGETHER, AND CUT OUT A HOLE.

5. TAPE THE THREE CARTONS TO THE TWO WHERE THE HOLE IS. USE LOTS OF TAPE FOR STRENGTH.

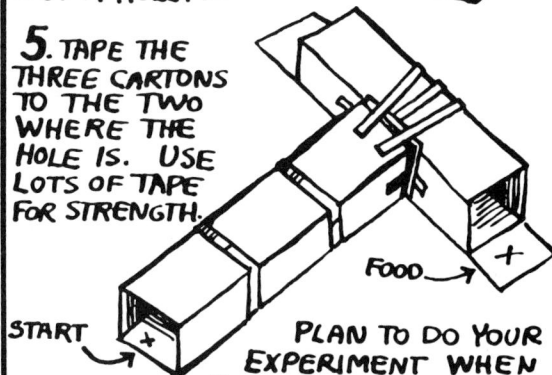

FOOD

START

PLAN TO DO YOUR EXPERIMENT WHEN YOUR RAT IS HUNGRY. PUT PEANUT BUTTER OR RAISINS ON ONE FLAP. PLACE THE RAT AT THE "START" END AND TIME ITS RUN TO THE FOOD. YOU CAN ALSO KEEP TRACK OF ANY WRONG TURNS.

BROWN RAT

BLACK RAT

soon learn which end has the food and go directly there to eat. Wait a day or two and try the experiment again. Keep the food in the same spot so you don't confuse your rat.

Some rats have short memories, but others will remember the right way for a long time. Once your rat has learned this simple T maze, you can use more milk cartons to make more complicated paths.

Rats Are Dangerous

Wild rats can be dangerous. Besides eating and spoiling our food, rats also carry diseases. The most fearsome is bubonic plague. Plague can now usually be cured with drugs, but people can still become very ill from it. Plague is carried from rat to rat and from rat to people by fleas. Several epidemics of plague have swept the world in times past.

Rats Are Helpful

Now that you know how dangerous rats are, it's only fair to say how important rats and mice are to medical research. Doctors test new drugs on mice and rats to see if the drugs are safe and helpful for people. Mice and rats can be used in research on drugs because these rodents get many of the same diseases as humans. Much of what we know about drugs, poisons, food additives, and good and bad diets we first learned from studies done with mice and rats.

A Mouse in the House

If you've ever had a mouse in your house, you know all about mouse signs. Mice leave little black droppings in the cup-

get into houses through holes around water and sewer pipes or through doors left open on warm summer evenings. Outdoors mice live under rocks, boards, and rubbish or in tunnels underground. Waste land or fields where house mice live will be full of tiny paths and tunnels through the grass.

Outdoor mice eat mainly seeds and a few types of insects. Indoor mice eat whatever is available: grain, cereal, bread, boards; they chew holes in the biscuit and cereal boxes; they hide their nests made of shredded paper, cloth, and string inside overstuffed couches and at the back of unused drawers. If you are sharp eyed, you might have caught a glimpse of a mouse as it zipped across the kitchen floor to hide behind the refrigerator.

The house mouse has followed people all over the world the way rats have. Besides living in houses, they also inhabit barns, warehouses, shops, fields, parks, and waste land. Indoors they can slip through the smallest cracks to live in walls and ceilings. They

MOUSE EXPERIMENTS

MICE (AND RATS TOO) ARE GOOD CLIMBERS. YOU CAN TEST THEIR CLIMBING ABILITY WITH A WIRE MESH LADDER.

1. CUT A LARGE SQUARE OF WIRE MESH WITH METAL CUTTERS.

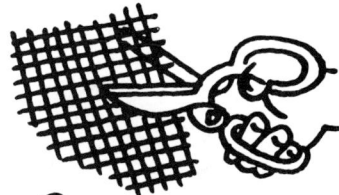

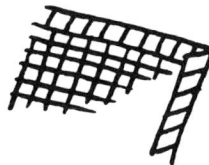

2. TURN THE SHARP EDGES UNDER WITH PLIERS SO YOU AND YOUR PET DON'T CUT YOURSELVES.

3. HOLD THE LADDER AT A SLANT AND START YOUR PET AT THE BOTTOM.

4. IF YOU START YOUR PET AT THE TOP, WHAT HAPPENS?

meat, and cheese. Mice travel only far enough to find food, nesting materials, and mates. A mouse that lives where the living is good might not travel much farther than the area of a large kitchen during its entire lifetime.

When a mouse does travel, it tries to stay hidden. Outdoors it runs through tunnels under the grass and leaves (or under the snow in winter). Indoors mice travel through walls and behind furniture. When a mouse does come out into the open, it tries to stay near cover. Mice have to be wary because something is usually out to catch them. Cats, dogs, people, hawks, owls, and weasels are always on the lookout for mice.

Keeping a Mouse

If you want to watch a mouse up close, the best thing to do is to buy a mouse at a pet store. They are easy to keep and feed. You need a metal cage that the mouse can't chew through. An exercise wheel for the mouse to run on is a good idea too. The mouse will make its own nest if you give it plenty of newspaper or old rags. It will help keep its cage clean by leaving droppings and urine in one corner, but you will have to help, too, by changing the newspaper every few days. Give your mouse water in a hanging water bottle (from the pet shop) and feed it seeds and nuts with treats of raisins, fruit, and meat scraps.

HOW TO MAKE A TIN TRAP FOR MICE

YOU NEED:

 A LARGE TIN

 A SNAP-TYPE MOUSETRAP

A PIECE OF WIRE MESH LARGE ENOUGH TO COVER THE END OF THE TIN.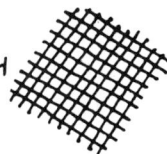

 A WOOD LOLLY STICK OR TONGUE DEPRESSOR TO HOLD BAIT.

SOME WIRE

METAL CUTTERS TO CUT THE WIRE.

A DRILL

TWO SHORT BOLTS WITH NUTS.

NEW BAIT STICK

DIRECTIONS:

1. CUT A CIRCLE OF WIRE MESH. IT SHOULD BE ABOUT 2.5 CM LARGER THAN THE END OF THE TIN ALL THE WAY AROUND.

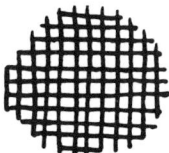

2. WIRE THE LOLLY STICK OR TONGUE DEPRESSOR ONTO THE BAIT PLATE OF THE TRAP.

3. BOLT THE MOUSE-TRAP ONTO THE OUTSIDE OF THE TIN. YOU'LL HAVE TO DRILL TWO HOLES THROUGH THE TRAP AND TIN FOR THIS. WHEN THE TRAP IS SET, THE SNAP PART SHOULD STICK OUT, BUT NOT TOO FAR. YOU WILL WANT IT TO HOLD THE WIRE MESH TIGHTLY AGAINST THE TIN WHEN THE TRAP IS SPRUNG.

4. WIRE THE CIRCLE OF WIRE MESH ONTO THE TRAP SNAP. YOU'LL HAVE TO CUT A NOTCH TO FIT IT OVER THE SPRING. IT HELPS TO HAVE SOMEONE HOLD IT FOR YOU SO YOU DON'T SNAP YOUR FINGERS.

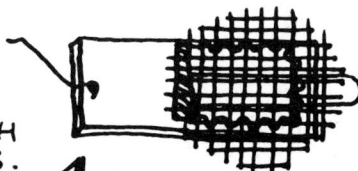

5. CHECK THE TRAP TO SEE THAT IT CLOSES TIGHTLY WITHOUT ANY GAPS.

6. SET THE TRAP AND TEST WITH A STICK TO SEE IF IT CAN BE SPRUNG EASILY WHEN THE BAIT STICK IS TOUCHED. YOU CAN ADJUST IT A LITTLE BY BENDING EITHER THE SETTING WIRE OR THE SETTING PLATE.

7. PUT PEANUT BUTTER ON THE BAIT STICK AND SET THE TRAP.

8. PLACE THE TRAP WHERE YOU EXPECT MICE TO BE.

SETTING WIRE HAS TO GO THROUGH THE WIRE MESH THEN OVER THE TOP.

CHECK THE TRAPS EVERY DAY. REMEMBER: WILD MICE AREN'T PETS AND THEY BITE. EITHER RELEASE THEM WITHOUT TOUCHING THEM OR WEAR HEAVY LEATHER GLOVES. MICE CAUGHT INDOORS CAN BE RELEASED IN WASTE LAND OR PARKS.

GOOD PLACES FOR MOUSETRAPS:

INDOORS: MICE RUN ALONG WALLS. TRAPS CAN BE SET THERE OR WHEREVER YOU FIND MOUSE DROPPINGS.

OUTDOORS: LOOK FOR MOUSE RUNS AND HOLES IN WASTE LAND AND WEEDY PLACES. TRAPS SHOULD BE PLACED RIGHT IN RUNS OR BESIDE HOLES. IF THE WEATHER IS COLD, OUTDOOR TRAPS SHOULD CONTAIN NESTING MATERIAL AND EXTRA FOOD SO THE MOUSE CAN KEEP WARM.

6
COCKROACHES AND DINOSAURS

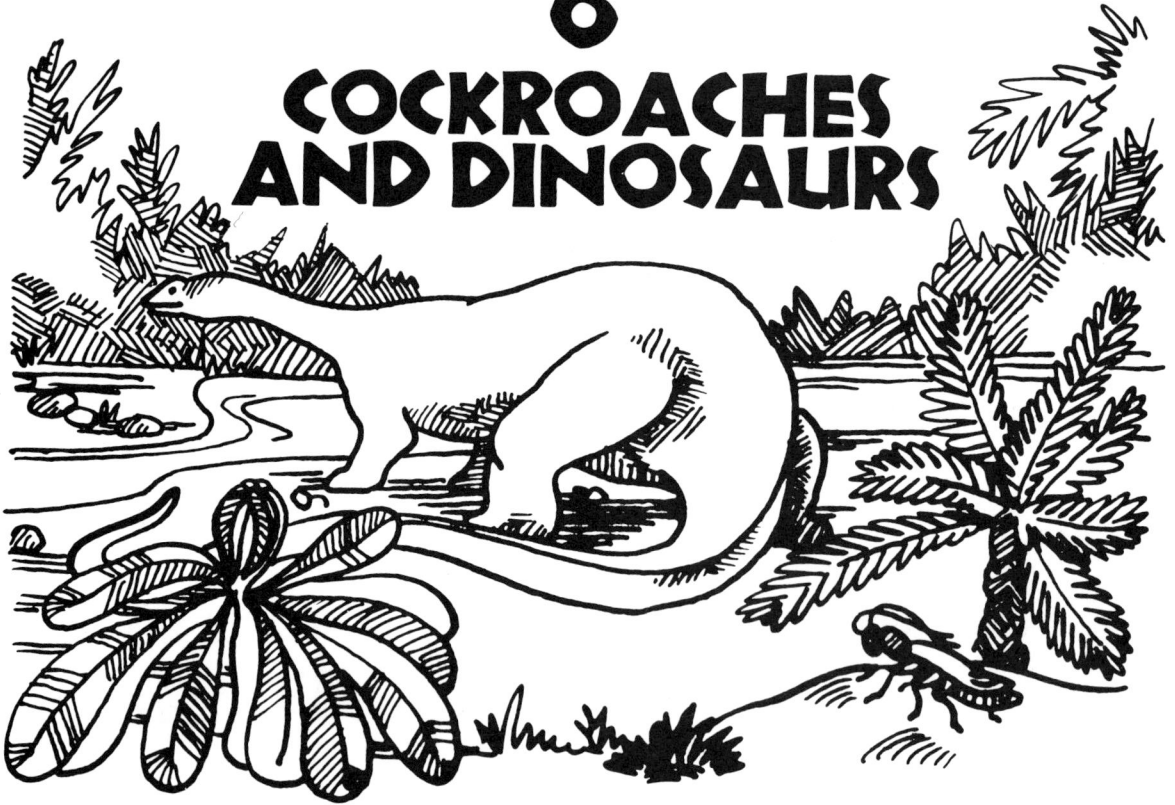

Cockroaches have been around for a long time. Most insects have changed a lot since the days of the dinosaurs, but not the cockroach. If dinosaurs were alive today, they'd recognize our cockroaches because they look nearly the same as the ones that scurried around the dinosaurs' feet millions of years ago. In fact, cockroaches are at least twice as ancient as the dinosaurs and go back 250 million years.

Today in Britain there are only a few kinds of cockroaches. Some live outdoors in the warmer southern counties. They can be found under bark and leaves and are not inclined to invade houses.

The three common house dwellers in Britain are called the American, German, and Common (Oriental) cockroaches. Although at one time they were thought to have come from those places, biological detective work shows that they probably all came from Africa. Like mice and rats, they have travelled with people to the far corners of the world. Now they live in people's houses and other places such as restaurants and supermarkets where there is plenty of food. Most people consider cockroaches to be very beastly neighbours, but read on. There's more to the cockroach than you think.

A Bathing Cockroach?

Does it surprise you to hear that cockroaches are clean? They often stop what they're doing to wash themselves, paying special attention to their antennae. If you keep a pet cockroach for a while, you can watch this cleaning behaviour. Even a newly caught cockroach, which is still nervous, will stop occasionally to run an antenna through its mouth to clean it.

The antennae on the head and the cerci on the cockroach's tail are very useful touch organs. They help the cockroach move around in dark places, whether it is going backwards or forwards.

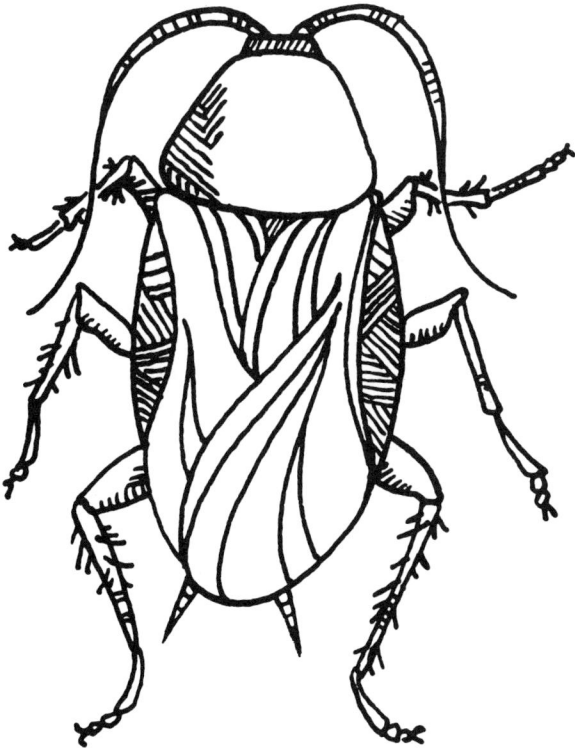

Besides the antennae and cerci, the body of an insect has groups of tiny hairs that keep it in touch with the outside world. Think of what it would be like if you lived inside a suit of armour. Your sense of touch and awareness of heat and cold would be greatly affected. The covering of an insect is a little like armour. Since insects don't have bones, their armour supports as well as protects them. Insects also need a sense of touch to tell them where they are and to warn them of danger. The tiny hairs reach out through the armour and provide a source of information about what's going on outside. In order for the hairs to do their job, they have to be clean and free of dust and dirt. Insects such as cockroaches and ants spend time in dusty places so they have to clean themselves regularly.

Any house can become invaded by cockroaches. They can slide through narrow crevices and come in through open windows and doors or along the outside of water and sewer pipes. The eggs can be brought home clinging to boxes or paper bags from a supermarket. Although supermarkets wage a constant war against cockroaches, there are always new ones coming in from warehouses or imported with goods shipped from other places.

Cockroach Pets

Cockroaches make good pets. They're small and can live comfortably in a jar. They eat almost anything. They don't bark or scratch the furniture. Also, for insects, they're relatively clever. You can even teach them to do tricks.

One of the first people to study cockroach behaviour was the biologist C. H. Turner. He found that a cockroach could learn to follow a maze back to its home jar. Turner's maze was a series of pathways set up over a tin of water so the cockroach couldn't escape. (You will learn how this works a little further on in this book.)

A JAR HOME

HOLES IN LID

CRUMPLED PAPER TOWEL
FRUIT
DOG FOOD

IS UP THE WAY OUT?

THIS IS THE EASIEST EXPERIMENT YOU CAN DO WITH AN INSECT.

1. FIRST CATCH A COCKROACH.

2. PUT IT IN A JAR AND PUT THE LID ON. (PUNCH HOLES IN THE LID IF YOU PLAN TO KEEP YOUR COCKROACH IN THERE FOR A WHILE.)

3. NOW WATCH YOUR COCKROACH AND SEE WHERE IT GOES.

4. TURN THE JAR UPSIDE DOWN AND WATCH.

5. LOOK AT A CLOCK AND SEE HOW LONG IT TAKES BEFORE THE COCKROACH BEGINS TO EXPLORE MORE THAN THE HIGHEST END OF THE JAR.

NOTE: THIS EXPERIMENT CAN BE DONE WITH OTHER INSECTS SUCH AS FLIES AND BEETLES.

Turner also taught cockroaches to avoid the dark. Cockroaches usually prefer the dark and stay away from the light. Turner used a box that was light on one side and dark on the other to study the cockroach's ability to learn. He found that if he gave the cockroaches an electric shock every time they went into the dark side of the box, they quickly learned to stay in the light side.

You can see for yourself if cockroaches prefer dark places by using the light-dark box described on page 37.

70

HOW TO MAKE A COCKROACH MAZE

YOU NEED:

A SHALLOW TIN OR BOWL
SEVERAL EMPTY PILL BOTTLES OR SMALL FILM CANISTERS
WATER
SAND OR PEBBLES TO ADD WEIGHT TO THE EMPTY BOTTLES
CARDBOARD STRIPS
BOOKS OR A BOX FOR SETTING THE HOME JAR BESIDE THE TIN

1. FILL THE BOTTLES WITH THE SAND OR PEBBLES.

2. ARRANGE THE BOTTLES IN THE TIN

3. LAY CARDBOARD STRIPS FROM ONE BOTTLE TO THE NEXT. ONE END OF THE MAZE SHOULD LEAD TO A DEAD END AND ONE SHOULD LEAD TO THE HOME JAR.

4. PUT 2.5 CM OF WATER IN THE TIN SO YOUR COCKROACH HAS TO STAY ON THE MAZE

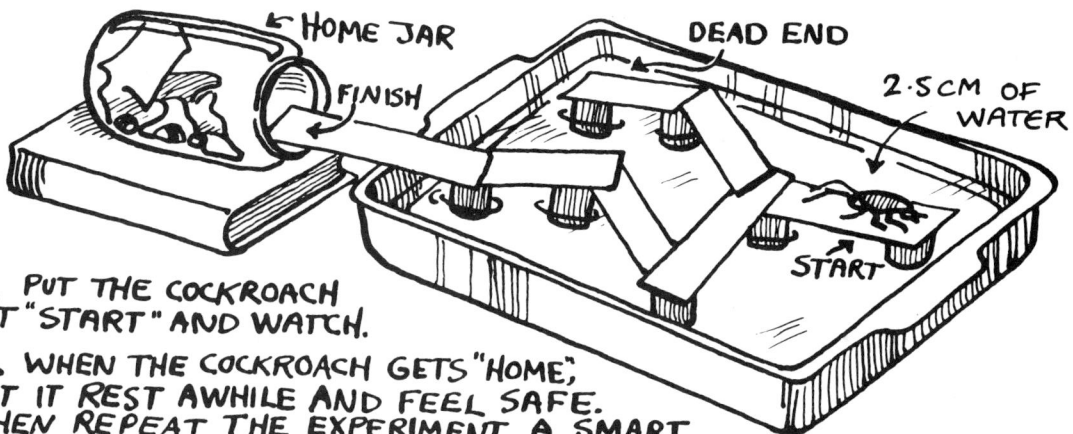

HOME JAR   DEAD END

FINISH   2.5 CM OF WATER

START

5. PUT THE COCKROACH AT "START" AND WATCH.

6. WHEN THE COCKROACH GETS "HOME", LET IT REST AWHILE AND FEEL SAFE. THEN REPEAT THE EXPERIMENT. A SMART COCKROACH WILL EVENTUALLY GO STRAIGHT HOME.

NOTE: SOME COCKROACHES CAN STILL REMEMBER THE WAY HOME THE NEXT DAY. OTHERS WILL FORGET.

Cockroach, Go Home!

You can do Turner's experiment to see how many tries it takes a cockroach to learn its way home over a maze. You will need a cockroach that has been living in the same jar for at least a few days so that it feels at home there.

Find a jam or pickle jar and make some holes with a nail in the jar lid. Crumple a paper towel into the jar for the cockroach to hide in. Now catch a cockroach. Feed your cockroach dry cereal, dog or cat food, and give it bits of fruit for moisture.

Now you are ready to build the maze.

A variation of this experiment is to use two cockroaches. Do you think they will help or hinder each other?

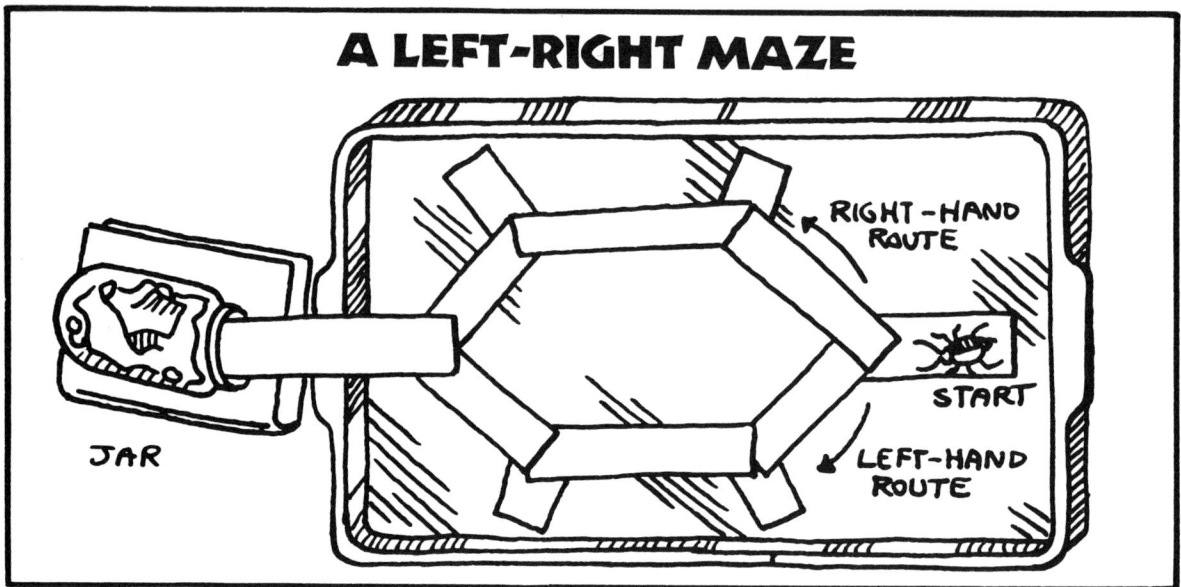

A LEFT-RIGHT MAZE

RIGHT-HAND ROUTE

START

LEFT-HAND ROUTE

JAR

Righty or Lefty?

Is your cockroach left-handed or right-handed? This can make a difference in the maze experiments. To test your cockroach, set up a maze with several left- and right-hand choices. Count how many left- or right-hand turns it makes. Then see if it learns a right- or left-turn maze faster. You can convince your friends that your cockroach is either smart or dumb once you learn which way it's most likely to turn.

7
CITY BIRDS

Many birds make their homes in the city. Even in inner-city areas, pigeons, blackbirds, and sparrows find nesting places in nooks in buildings and in the trees of small parks. At lunch time they feed on leftovers from people. These birds are especially dependent on us. If buildings didn't have crevices and ledges, if we didn't plant street trees and make places for small parks, if we didn't drop food from our lunches, these birds could not live in cities; and some of the nicest "beasts" around would not be our neighbours.

Bird Restaurants

The best way to get close to birds is to feed them. A window feeder is simple to make, and once birds learn to come to it, you can watch them right through the window. Move slowly and quietly and the birds will ignore you as they hop about having dinner.

Almost any window can have a bird feeder in it, even one that is high up in a block of flats. If there are trees nearby, birds will probably find your feeder quickly. But even if you live on the sixth floor of a block of flats, birds will find you. Have patience, put out food regularly, and soon the birds will come to you.

MAKE A WINDOW FEEDER

YOU NEED:

A BOARD 1-2 CM THICK, 20 OR 30 CM WIDE, AND 30 CM OR MORE LONG (IT CAN BE AS LONG AS YOUR WINDOWSILL)

A STICK OR A PIECE OF WOOD ABOUT 2 CM SQUARE AND AS LONG AS YOUR BOARD

NAILS AND A HAMMER

1. NAIL THE STICK TO ONE EDGE OF THE BOARD TO KEEP THE SEED FROM ROLLING OFF YOUR FEEDER.

2. NAIL (OR WIRE) THE BOARD TO YOUR WINDOWSILL.

Dry Food

If it snows where you live in winter or if it rains a lot, this feeder is a good one to make. You can either find a wooden fruit box or make your own. Apples and pears are sometimes shipped in wooden boxes, so ask at your greengrocers.

Nail the box to a post or tree where you can see it from your window. You can also use this box as a window feeder if you cut a hole in the back (really the bottom of the box) so you can see the birds and reach in to add food.

The Menu

You can buy bird seed in the pet department of most supermarkets and at pet shops. Birds will also eat bread and biscuit crumbs; dry cereal; uncooked oatmeal or rice; raisins; cut-up pieces of apple, pear, and banana; sunflower seeds; and nuts. You can try putting out other foods for them as well. If you're curious about what the birds like best, put the food into jar lids and see which ones they empty first.

It is important not to close the "restaurant" suddenly. Your birds will be depending on you for food. In winter they may starve to death if you stop feeding them. Put out food at the same time every day. If you know you are going to be away for a few days in winter, ask someone else to feed your birds and explain why it's important. Plan ahead. You can encourage your birds to find new places to eat if you feed them less and less each day for a week before you go away. Then they will have time to find new food sources.

A FEEDER WITH A ROOF

TO MAKE A ROOFED FEEDER YOU NEED:

NAILS, A HAMMER, AND A SAW
A BOARD 30 CM WIDE, 96 CM LONG AND 1 CM THICK

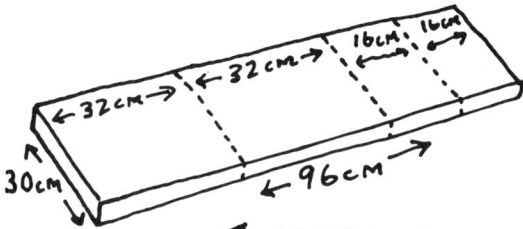

1. CUT TWO PIECES 32 CM LONG.

2. CUT TWO PIECES 16 CM LONG.

3. NAIL THE SHORT PIECES BETWEEN THE ENDS OF THE LONG ONES.

NOTE: IF YOU USE SCREWS, YOUR FEEDER WILL BE STRONGER, BUT YOU'LL NEED TO DRILL HOLES TO GET THE SCREWS STARTED. GET SOMEONE TO HELP YOU, AND USE A DRILL BIT THAT'S JUST A LITTLE SMALLER THAN YOUR SCREWS.

4. YOU CAN SAND AND PAINT THE OUTSIDE OF YOUR FEEDER, BUT THE BIRDS WILL BE JUST AS HAPPY IF YOU LEAVE IT.

5. NAIL (OR WIRE) THE FEEDER TO YOUR WINDOWSILL, OR FASTEN IT TO A TREE, AND YOU'RE IN BUSINESS: THE RESTAURANT BUSINESS FOR BIRDS, THAT IS!

More Bird Feeders

Mix bird seed with peanut butter and fill the spaces in a pine cone with it. Tie a string around the pine cone and hang it outside near a window.

Some kinds of cheese, onion, and grapes come wrapped in plastic or string net bags. Save these bags for suet holders. Ask for beef suet in the meat department of a supermarket. Wrap it in the net bag and hang it up for the birds.

Water to Drink

Water is sometimes scarce in cities and towns. Streams often run through underground pipes, and ponds are filled in and drained so that houses can be built on top of them. Offer your birds some drinking water in jar lids or shallow dishes. You can set a dish of water right on your bird feeder.

Bath time!

Birds love to take baths. The easiest bath to make is an old dustbin lid turned upside down. Balance the lid on a mound of soil or on top of some rocks. Put flat rocks or pebbles in the bottom to give the birds something to stand on. The water should be about 2·5 cm deep for most birds.

The best place to put a bird bath is near (but not up against) a low tree or bush. There should be an open area around the bath so cats can't sneak up on it. Wet birds can't fly very well. The bush or tree gives them a safe place to sit while they preen (straighten and smooth) their feathers and wait for them to get dry.

A Place to Live

Some birds nest in tree branches or bushes. We help these birds by planting trees and creating parks and gardens. Other birds nest in holes or on ledges. In the wild they use holes in dead trees or ledges on rocky cliffs. People usually cut down dead trees and remove dead branches. This leaves the birds without places to nest. Many areas would have more birds if there were nesting spots for them.

General Birdhouse

This birdhouse is designed to be made from just one board of wood measuring roughly 15 cm wide, 1 cm thick and 150 cm long. You might find a plank already cut to this size at your local timber yard.

Birdwatchers who want to attract special birds build their birdhouses to exact measurements. The birds themselves are not usually quite so fussy. When nature hollows out a tree, the cavity is seldom exactly a certain number of centimetres each way, and the hole isn't exact either. The house described here can be used by several kinds of birds. It's large enough for a sparrow, but a bluetit might use it too. If you live in the city, you probably don't have bluetits, but you probably

AN ALL-AROUND BIRDHOUSE

MATERIALS:
A BOARD 15 CM WIDE
1 CM THICK AND 150 CM LONG
A SAW   NAILS AND A HAMMER
A HINGE   A DRILL AND DRILL BITS
A PENCIL   A KEYHOLE SAW
A RULER   OR A HOLE-CUTTING
ATTACHMENT FOR
THE POWER
DRILL.

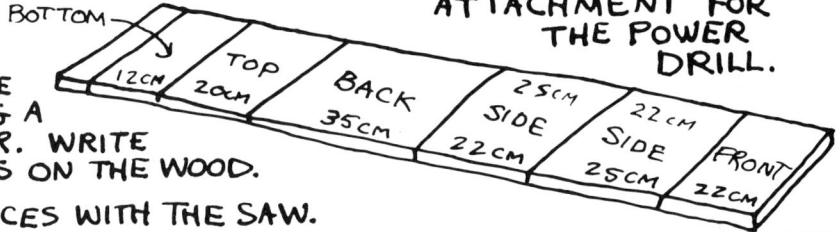

BOTTOM — 12CM   TOP 20CM   BACK 35CM   SIDE 22CM 25CM   SIDE 25CM 22 CM   FRONT 22CM

1. MARK THE WHOLE BOARD FIRST, USING A PENCIL AND A RULER. WRITE WHAT EACH PIECE IS ON THE WOOD.

2. CUT OUT THE PIECES WITH THE SAW.

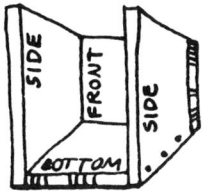

3. NAIL THE FRONT TO THE BOTTOM.

4. NAIL ON THE SIDES. NOTICE THAT THE FRONT GOES OVER THE SIDES, AND THE BOTTOM FITS INSIDE WHERE YOU CAN'T SEE IT.

5. NAIL ON THE BACK.

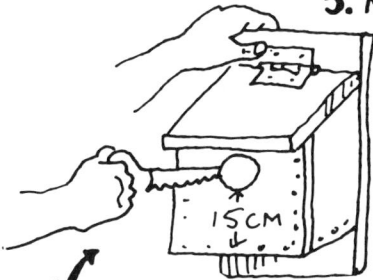

6. PUT THE ROOF ON AND ATTACH THE HINGE. NOTICE THAT THE LID IS FASTENED ONLY BY THE HINGE. THIS WILL LET YOU CLEAN OUT THE BOX WHEN THE BIRDS ARE FINISHED WITH IT. (YOU CAN ALSO PEEK INSIDE TO SEE THE BABIES WHEN THE PARENTS ARE AWAY, BUT DON'T DO THIS WHEN THEY ARE BUILDING OR HAVE EGGS BECAUSE THEY MIGHT NOT COME BACK.)

7. CUT THE DOOR. MAKE IT ABOUT 15 CM FROM THE FLOOR AND ABOUT 5 CM IN DIAMETER. THE EASIEST WAY TO CUT THIS ROUND DOOR IS WITH A HOLE-CUTTING ATTACHMENT TO A POWER DRILL, (HAVE AN ADULT HELP), OR YOU CAN USE A KEYHOLE SAW. DRILL A SMALL HOLE TO GET IT STARTED.

15CM

8. DRILL TWO SMALL HOLES ON EACH SIDE JUST UNDER THE ROOF FOR VENTILATION. DRILL FOUR <u>SMALL</u> HOLES IN THE FLOOR FOR DRAINAGE IN CASE WATER GETS INSIDE.

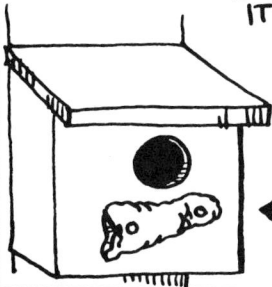

9. YOU CAN PAINT THE <u>OUTSIDE</u> ONLY, (DON'T PAINT THE INSIDE) OR LEAVE THE WOOD NATURAL. IF YOU DO PAINT, CHOOSE A COLOUR THAT BLENDS WITH THE ENVIRONMENT. NAIL A ROUGH PIECE OF BARK JUST UNDER THE HOLE TO GIVE THE BIRDS A FIRM FOOTING.

10. NAIL YOUR BIRDHOUSE TO A TREE OR POST. A SHADY SPOT IS BEST. HOUSES IN THE SUN CAN HEAT UP LIKE OVENS ON A WARM DAY. BIRDHOUSES CAN ALSO BE FASTENED TO WINDOWSILLS (NOT BESIDE A FEEDER) OR UNDER THE EAVES OF A HOUSE.

do have sparrows. Some people don't like these birds and don't build houses they can use, but to some of us all birds are interesting to watch, and if you can watch them bring up a family, that's even more interesting.

An Observation Birdhouse

Build the same house, but don't put on a back. Instead, nail on the roof and leave the back open. Tape the house to your window (use heavy duty tape from a builder's merchant's), so you can see right inside it.

The only problem with an observation house is that you won't be able to use the window during nesting season. To get the birds to use the house, the window must be covered so the birds can't see people on the other side. If there aren't curtains on the window, cover it with black paper, heavy cloth, or cardboard, except where the birdhouse is. Fasten a piece of dark material over the birdhouse part of the window so you can lift it up to peek into the house. There should be enough so that you can drape it over your head. Imagine using an old-fashioned view camera behind which the photographer ducks under a black cloth to look through the lens and you will have the idea. The trick is to see the birds without their seeing you.

Ledge Nests for Pigeons and Doves

When a pigeon or dove builds a nest, it gathers a few sticks together and drops them in a loose pile. Pigeons put their sticks on ledges. In the wild they look for rocky cliffs. In the city they look for level building decorations. Doves build better nests than pigeons do. They weave a few sticks together on a flat tree branch or lay sticks between two branches that are growing close together. If pigeons and doves live in your neighbourhood, you can help them with their nest building and watch them raise their chicks.

MAKE A LEDGE NEST

PIGEONS WILL BUILD ON A WINDOWSILL IF THERE IS ENOUGH ROOM AND THE WINDOW IS HIGH ENOUGH (GENERALLY SECOND FLOOR OR HIGHER). A BOARD WITH 2.5 CM-HIGH SIDES CAN BE NAILED OR WIRED TO A WINDOWSILL FOR PIGEONS.

YOU NEED:

A BOARD 20 CM WIDE, 30 CM LONG, AND 1 CM THICK
A PIECE OF WOOD 2.5 CM SQUARE AND 90 CM LONG
A SAW, NAILS, AND A HAMMER
A PENCIL AND RULER

30CM   30CM   15CM   15CM

1. MARK THE 2.5 CM BY 2.5 CM WOOD WITH A PENCIL AND RULER. YOU NEED TWO PIECES 30 CM LONG AND TWO PIECES 15 CM LONG.

2. SAW THE WOOD INTO THE LENGTHS YOU MARKED.

3. NAIL THE STRIPS ONTO THE BOARD TO MAKE A SHALLOW BOX.

4. NAIL OR WIRE IT TO A WINDOWSILL.

Collared Dove Nest

Sometimes doves have a hard time finding two close branches or a level one on which to build their nests. A small, flat basket or wood platform will give them a place to build. The platform can be made from strips of wood nailed between two branches close together. The basket can be nailed right to a larger branch. Doves usually nest on low branches, so you don't have to climb far up into a tree. Watch to see where the doves spend their time and put the nest support nearby.

Home on the Roof

Some birds don't build a fancy nest out of twigs and grasses. Instead they scrape out a shallow spot on bare ground and lay their eggs among stones. The speckled eggs look so much like small rocks, they're almost impossible to see. In cities, where roads, pavements, and houses take up most of the space, some ground-nesting birds have found new pebble patches to use for nests: they build on rooftops. Flat tar and gravel roofs are often the next best thing to a gravelly patch of ground. They may even be safer. People and other animals aren't likely to step on a rooftop nest, and cats and dogs aren't likely to find it and eat the eggs.

79

Common rooftop nesters in seaside towns and cities are herring gulls and lesser black-backed gulls. They nest happily on flat roofs, in nooks where the nest is held securely, and even on chimney stacks between the pots.

They generally scavenge for food around the harbours and fish docks, and at the local refuse tips and sewage outfalls.

screeching noisily around the rooftops.

Swifts also commonly nest in towns. They originally nested in holes in trees but find holes in buildings suitable too. They do almost everything whilst flying, including feeding, mating, even sleeping.

They are attracted to towns by the abundance of flying insects which they catch whilst

Treetop Nests

Tree nesters stand out because their nests are easy to see. Many birds hide their nests in dense shrubbery where they are hard to find. Wood pigeons, crows and mistle thrushes, however, build up in trees where we can usually see their nests.

There are several ways to find tree nests.

1. Search each tree, looking for collections of twigs or a dark dense place in the branches.
2. Listen for peeping baby birds. When a parent arrives at the nest with food, the chicks are often very noisy.
3. Watch any bird you see carrying nesting material (such as sticks or grass) or food (such as insects or worms) in its beak. When a bird has a mouthful, it will head for its nest.
4. Be patient! Most birds don't fly directly to their nest, but

take a roundabout route. This helps protect the nest from predators. Once you've discovered the pattern, you'll see the same bird use it again and again. 5. If you are suddenly dive-bombed by a lesser black-backed gull, you know there's a nest nearby. Move away a little and watch the bird. It will be defending the territory around its nest.

FEED A BIRD FROM YOUR HAND

DID YOU EVER WISH YOU COULD TAME A BIRD SO IT WOULD SIT RIGHT ON YOUR HAND? YOU CAN DO IT IF YOU ARE PATIENT AND QUIET, AND IF YOU KNOW A LITTLE TRICK. YOU SHOULD TRY THIS IN THE WINTER WHEN THE BIRDS ARE VERY HUNGRY AND ARE ALREADY COMING TO YOUR WINDOWSILL FEEDER EVERY DAY. YOU WILL NEED:

A GLOVE

AN OLD SHIRT OR COAT SLEEVE

A STICK

NEWSPAPER OR RAGS

1. MAKE A SCARECROW-TYPE ARM BY PUTTING THE STICK INTO THE SLEEVE AND GLOVE, THEN STUFFING THE WHOLE THING WITH CRUMPLED NEWSPAPER.

2. FASTEN THE ARM SECURELY TO YOUR WINDOWSILL FEEDER WITH THE END OF THE ARM UNDER THE WINDOW.

3. PUT FOOD ON THE GLOVE EVERY DAY. AT FIRST THE BIRDS WILL BE AFRAID, BUT SINCE IT'S THERE ALL THE TIME, EVENTUALLY THEY WILL ACCEPT IT AS PART OF THE FEEDER.

4. WHEN THE BIRDS ARE <u>VERY</u> USED TO IT AND WILL SIT AND EAT SEED FROM THE GLOVE, YOU ARE READY TO SWITCH HANDS. TAKE OUT THE STICK AND PAPER AND SLIDE YOUR OWN HAND INSIDE THE GLOVE. SIT <u>VERY</u> STILL AND DON'T LOOK DIRECTLY AT THE BIRDS. KEEP THE WINDOW CLOSED EXCEPT FOR YOUR ARM AND <u>HAVE PATIENCE</u>!

5. WHEN YOUR ARM ISN'T IN THE SLEEVE, MAKE UP THE FAKE ONE AGAIN AND PUT IT BACK OUT. AFTER A WEEK OR TWO WHEN THE BIRDS ARE MORE USED TO YOUR HAND INSIDE THE GLOVE, TRY TAKING IT OFF. PUT THE FOOD ON YOUR HAND. REMEMBER, EACH CHANGE WILL WORRY THE BIRDS, SO HAVE PATIENCE. <u>DON'T</u> TRY TO CATCH THE BIRDS OR PET THEM. YOUR <u>OPEN</u> HAND IS OKAY, BUT IF THEY EVER THINK YOU MIGHT GRAB THEM, THEY COULD BECOME AFRAID OF YOU FOREVER.

8
WEEDS CAN BE BEAUTIFUL

A weed is just a plant out of place, growing where someone doesn't want it. Plants that some people think are weeds are planted and cultivated for their flowers by other people. And sometimes we are glad to have weeds; for example, the dandelions and couch grass we don't want growing in our lawns may be the only green things growing on waste land. Weeds look especially good when they grow where nothing else will. The edges of roads and car parks and old industrial areas are havens for weeds. Weeds are good to have around when they brighten our lives with their green leaves and colourful flowers, and when they attract butterflies, birds, and other animals.

Plants in Odd Places

Where is the most unusual place you've ever seen a plant growing? Was it a crack in a pavement or a rain gutter on a roof? Many plants have seeds that will sprout almost anywhere. A little moisture is all that's needed because the seed contains food enough for the young plant to begin growing. If the plant is to grow long enough to make flowers and produce seed, it needs more food than its seed contains. Plants get their food from soil and dead decaying plants, and if this food isn't available, the plant soon dies.

To find out how plants growing in strange places survive, look into a pavement crack. Cracks in

82

cement, crevices in buildings, holes in fences, and rain gutters are natural traps for wind-blown soil and leaves: everything a plant needs to grow and be healthy.

Here's a game to play either by yourself or with a friend. As you walk along, look for plants growing in unusual places and count points for the most unusual.

YOU CAN KEEP SCORE FOR A CERTAIN DISTANCE OR FOR A LIMITED AMOUNT OF TIME.

THE GROWING PLANT GAME

SCORE 1 POINT FOR EACH LEAFY PLANT GROWING IN A CRACK.

SCORE 2 POINTS FOR EACH FLOWERING PLANT GROWING IN A CRACK.

SCORE 5 POINTS FOR A PLANT GROWING OUT OF SOME PLACE ABOVE THE GROUND, SUCH AS A FENCE OR A ROOF.

SCORE 10 POINTS FOR A PLANT GROWING ON A MOVING OBJECT, SUCH AS A CAR.

IF YOU WALK THE SAME WAY EVERY DAY, SEE IF YOU CAN BEAT YOUR OLD SCORE AS YOU GET BETTER AT SPOTTING PLANTS.

Walk for Seeds

Plan to take this walk in summer or autumn when most plants, especially weeds, will have ripe seeds. The idea is to collect as many different kinds of seeds on your socks as you can. This is your chance to show your own brother or sister something about weeds. Or take all your friends along.

SOCK WALK

YOU NEED A LARGE PAIR OF OLD SOCKS FOR EACH PERSON.

1. FIND WEEDY WASTE LAND OR A PARK OR FIELD.

2. PUT THE OLD SOCKS ON OVER YOUR SHOES.

3. WALK AROUND AMONG THE PLANTS.

4. SIT DOWN, TAKE OFF YOUR OLD SOCKS, AND PICK THE SEEDS OFF THEM.

5. MAKE PILES OF THE DIFFERENT KINDS OF SEEDS AND SEE HOW MANY YOU FOUND.

6. IMAGINE WHAT WOULD HAPPEN IF YOUR SOCKS WERE A RABBIT'S FOOT OR A FOX'S TAIL.

7. TAKE EACH SEED AND TRY TO FIND THE KIND OF PLANT IT CAME FROM.

PLANT DETECTIVE GAME

YOU AND YOUR FRIENDS CAN BE PLANT DETECTIVES. THE OBJECT OF THE GAME IS TO DESCRIBE A SECRET PLANT SO WELL THAT SOMEONE ELSE CAN FIND IT JUST BY READING YOUR DESCRIPTION.

YOU NEED:
TWO OR MORE PLAYERS
PAPER AND PENCIL FOR EACH PLAYER

1. CHOOSE A MEETING SPOT (GOAL).

2. EACH PERSON TAKES PAPER AND PENCIL AND GOES AWAY TO FIND A SECRET PLANT.

3. SIT DOWN BESIDE YOUR PLANT AND LOOK AT IT CAREFULLY. SMELL IT, TOUCH IT, SEE WHERE IT GROWS.

4. WRITE A DESCRIPTION OF YOUR PLANT. THESE ARE CLUES TO HELP A DETECTIVE FIND IT, SO MAKE IT AS COMPLETE AS YOU CAN.

5. GO BACK TO THE GOAL AND WAIT FOR YOUR FRIENDS. WHEN EVERYONE IS THERE, TRADE CLUES.

6. TAKE YOUR NEW CLUES AND TRY TO FIND THE PLANT. WHEN YOU THINK YOU'VE FOUND IT, ASK THE DESCRIBER IF YOU'RE RIGHT (NO HINTS EXCEPT FOR WHAT'S WRITTEN).

7. WHEN YOU'VE FOUND IT, GO BACK TO THE GOAL. THE FIRST PERSON TO FIND THE RIGHT PLANT AND REACH THE GOAL IS THE WINNER.

<u>NOTE</u>: WITH FOUR OR MORE PEOPLE, YOU CAN HAVE TWO WINNERS EACH TIME: THE DETECTIVE <u>AND</u> THE DESCRIBER. THE BEST CLUES HELP THE DETECTIVE.

HOW TO PLANT A WEED

SAVE THE SEEDS FROM YOUR SOCK WALK, OR GO OUT AND COLLECT NEW ONES. IF YOU'RE NOT SOCK-WALKING, YOU CAN GATHER WIND-BLOWN SEEDS SUCH AS DANDELION, WILLOWHERB AND GROUNDSEL.

YOU NEED PLANT POTS SUCH AS PAPER CUPS, EMPTY MILK OR EGG CARTONS, AND SOIL. POTTING SOIL IS BEST BUT DARK GARDEN SOIL IS OKAY.

1. PUNCH HOLES IN THE PLANT POTS FOR DRAINAGE.

2. FILL PLANT POTS 3/4 FULL OF SOIL (LEAVE ROOM FOR WATERING).

3. WATER THE SOIL FIRST. NEW POTTING SOIL IS HARD TO WET, SO STIR IT WELL.

4. PLANT YOUR SEEDS. PUT SEVERAL SEEDS OF THE SAME KIND IN EACH PLANT POT

5. PUT THE PLANT POTS IN A SUNNY SPOT AND WATER REGULARLY. FEEL THE SOIL; IF IT'S DRY, ADD WATER; IF IT'S WET, WAIT.

AT FIRST, BABY PLANTS LOOK A LOT ALIKE. YOUR PLANTS WILL LOOK MORE INTERESTING AS THEY GROW UP. SOME WEEDS ARE QUITE BEAUTIFUL, ESPECIALLY WHEN THEIR FLOWERS APPEAR.

BINDWEED

WILD SWEET PEA

DANDELION

SOME SEEDS YOU MAY FIND

BURDOCK

SYCAMORE

AGRIMONY

DANDELION

GOOSE GRASS

9
HOW ANIMALS SURVIVE IN THE CITY

People have changed the environment of cities and towns so much that animals often find it hard to live in them. They have trouble finding food and shelter. They risk being run over by cars when they cross streets. They risk being chased or eaten by dogs and cats, which are more numerous than predators in the wild.

In spite of these problems, a surprisingly large number of wild animals live in cities, and even more live in towns and suburbs. Many cities have bats, and owls. City parks often have ducks and rabbits, not to mention squirrels. Some large parks even have foxes. All these animals depend on people in one way or another. People decide where the parks will be and what they will look like. The animals need wild areas of bushes and trees set aside for them in parks and gardens. They need food, nesting places, and water. You can help them.

One of the easiest ways to help animals is to plant something. Plant a bush or a tree and let a bit of your garden grow wild. If you plant a bush that has berries, you will also be feeding the animals. Mulberry, hawthorn, firethorn, and rose are good food-bearing trees and bushes to plant.

Being a Tramp as a Way of Life

The world is full of animal tramps who have found that looking for handouts is an easy way of living. Of course, people encourage them to do this by providing food. You probably know some animal tramps, especially if you feed birds or squirrels. Parks where people eat their lunches are great places for animal tramps.

Animals that rely mostly on people for food often become tame. Pigeons learn to walk right under your feet after scraps and bread crumbs; squirrels climb up onto your shoulder after peanuts. One thing you should remember about these animals: they are "tame" because they aren't afraid of you and they're hungry. They aren't tame the same way a pet hamster or cat is. A friendly squirrel may very well bite you if you try to pet or touch it, even if it has just taken food from your hand.

The saddest animal tramps in cities aren't the wild creatures that need our handouts, but dogs and cats that don't have owners. Pets that have gone wild because people have abandoned them are called "feral" animals. There are many of them in every city and town. People who get tired of a dog or cat, or who move away, often set their pets free to take care of themselves. What feral dogs and cats are really free to do is to slowly starve or to die from disease.

Wild animals that depend on people for food often don't get a balanced diet. Birds are probably the least affected because they fly from one place to another and eat berries and insects as well as the food people give them. Rubbish, crisps, and bread are not a balanced diet for most wild animals. In the wild they would eat nuts, insects, worms, berries, and many other foods. The best we can do if we feed them is to offer a variety of things.

There are always more questions than answers when it comes to feeding wild animals. Do we encourage them to depend on us too much? Are we

responsible for feeding them because we've changed their environment by eliminating their sources of adequate natural food? Could any of these wild animals live in cities if we didn't help them?

Inner-city Watering Holes

A good place to look for wild animals and birds is near water. You can find their tracks in the mud around the edges of ponds, streams, and springs. In the evening you can often see the animals themselves when they come to get a drink. Stone-age people knew this, and much of their hunting was done near water. Animals are creatures of habit; evening after evening they will come to the same place to drink.

In cities and towns water is often hard to find today. If you can find an old map or photograph of your neighbourhood, look to see if it once had streams or springs that are now gone. Towns and even suburbs have the bad habit of putting streams into underground pipes and of filling marshy areas and building shopping centres on them. Once the water is underground, the animals have lost a place to drink, and you've lost a place to watch them.

Water for wildlife is easy to supply. All you need is a container, which can be anything from an old dustbin lid to a cement-lined pool. You could use an old dustbin lid turned upside down and set on stones or bricks, a big plastic bowl or old pots or dishes.

If you use a container that has high sides, like an old plastic baby bath, you will need to sink it into the ground or build up stones around it. Small animals such as mice can fall into deep containers and drown. To prevent this you can put in a wood float or pile stones in one end so they can climb out.

Keep containers filled with clean water. If foxes come to visit, they will muddy the water by washing food and playing in it, so you might need to change it every day.

The Fishing Is Great in a Garden Pond

People with ponds sometimes find they have animals they hadn't planned to have. A heron can quickly eat all the fish in a small garden pond. These birds are fun to watch, if you don't mind feeding them your fish.

Plant Your Pond

Look for plants growing in or beside ponds and streams in the country and bring some home in plastic bags. You could also buy plants at an aquarium shop. Some good plants for garden ponds are floating plants such as water fern and duckweed, and rooted plants such as Canadian

A GARDEN POND

HERE'S AN EASY WAY TO MAKE A POND.
YOU NEED:
A LARGE CONTAINER
SUCH AS A HALF-BARREL OF WOOD,
A SMALL PLASTIC DUSTBIN,
A METAL WASH-TUB,
AN OLD BATHTUB,
OR AN OLD KITCHEN SINK.

1. FOR AN OLD TUB OR SINK, PLUG THE OUTLET WITH A GOOD, TIGHT RUBBER PLUG.

2. A WOODEN TUB THAT HAS DRIED OUT WILL LEAK AT FIRST. FILL IT WITH WATER EVERY DAY, AND EVENTUALLY THE WOOD WILL SWELL AND HOLD WATER. HAVE FAITH. WOOD SWELLS A LOT, AND EVENTUALLY IT SHOULD LEAK ONLY A LITTLE.

pondweed, water lily, and watercress.

Note: Plants rooted in soil can be grown in flowerpots. First put the plant in soil in a flowerpot, then set the pot down into the water in your pond.

Animals for Your Pond

When your pond has plants growing in it, insects will come

PLANTS AND ANIMALS FOR YOUR POND

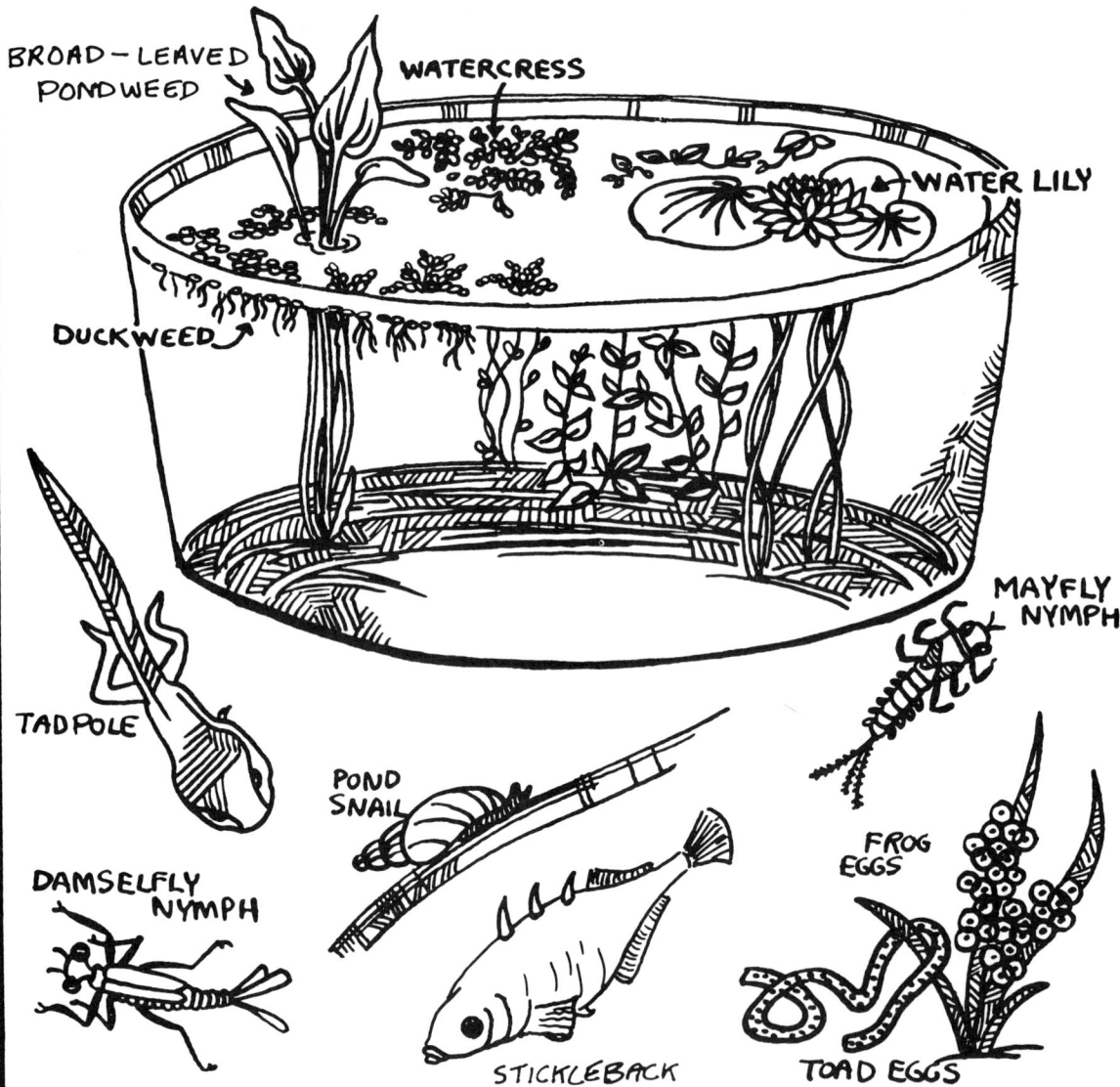

BROAD-LEAVED PONDWEED

WATERCRESS

WATER LILY

DUCKWEED

MAYFLY NYMPH

TADPOLE

POND SNAIL

FROG EGGS

DAMSELFLY NYMPH

STICKLEBACK

TOAD EGGS

and lay their eggs there. Before that happens, you can introduce insects from a natural pond. Don't catch stream insects. They usually need more oxygen than your pond will have.

If your garden has a place for frogs and toads, you can breed tadpoles in your pond.

Two or three small goldfish from the pet shop or a few sticklebacks will keep mosquitoes in check by eating their eggs and larvae. If your pond has plenty of insects in it, a few small fish will not need extra food during the summer.

Snails do well in small ponds.

Look for them in country ponds or buy them at a pet shop.

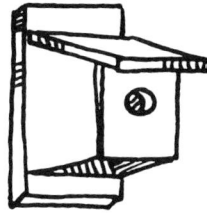
NEST BOXES

Hollow Tree for Rent

City animals sometimes live in the strangest places. Robins nest in overturned flowerpots, sparrows build nests in holes in walls, and bats roost in old roofs. Most of these animals would live in hollow trees in the wild, but hollow trees are scarce in cities and towns, so they look for the next best thing. There's a lot you can do to help animals find places to live. You can:

BUSHES

1. Build nest boxes of different sizes and put them in trees or next to your house.

2. Plant bushes that will grow thick and make a good place to crawl under.

PLANT A TREE

3. Plant a tree; a good choice would be an oak or maple that will grow tall and live for a long time.

ROCK AND LOG PILE

4. Build a loose pile of logs or rocks. The spaces in between them make good homes for mice, toads, and insects.

5. Leave piles of leaves in the corners of your garden. Toads, hedgehogs, and soil animals will live under leaves, and the leaves will enrich the soil.

LEAF PILE

6. Turn part of your garden into a nature reserve by letting the weeds and grass grow tall. Weedy places make wonderful hideouts for small animals.

NATURE RESERVE

MAKE A NEST BOX FOR SQUIRRELS

SQUIRRELS BUILD LEAFY NESTS HIGH IN THE BRANCHES OF TALL TREES. THEY ALSO LIKE TO NEST INSIDE HOLLOW TREES, ESPECIALLY DURING VERY COLD OR RAINY WEATHER. THIS NEST BOX CAN BE USED BY SQUIRRELS OR OWLS.

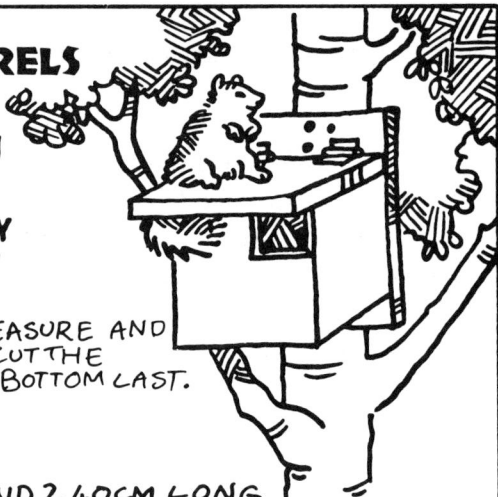

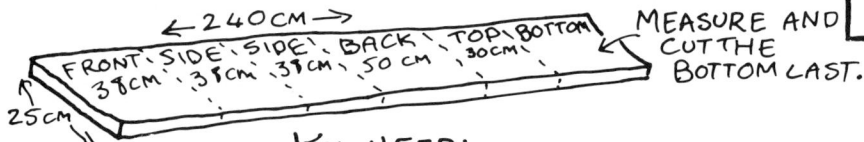

← 240 CM →

FRONT · SIDE · SIDE · BACK · TOP · BOTTOM
38 CM · 35 CM · 35 CM · 50 CM · 30 CM

25 CM

MEASURE AND CUT THE BOTTOM LAST.

YOU NEED:

A BOARD 25 CM WIDE, 1 CM THICK, AND 240 CM LONG.
2 HINGES   NAILS AND A HAMMER
A SAW AND DRILL   PENCIL AND RULER

1. MARK THE BOARD WITH PENCIL AND RULER. WRITE ON EACH PIECE SO YOU'LL KNOW WHAT IT IS AFTER IT'S CUT.

2. CUT OUT ALL OF THE PIECES.

3. CUT AN 8 CM BY 8 CM HOLE FROM ONE CORNER OF THE FRONT FOR AN ENTRANCE.

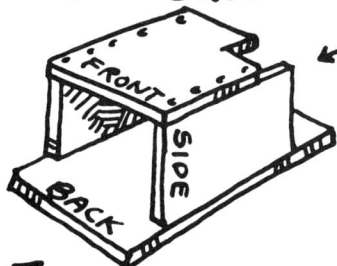

4. NAIL THE FRONT AND THE SIDES TOGETHER.

5. NAIL THE BACK ON. IT SHOULD STICK UP ABOVE THE TOP OF THE BOX.

6. MEASURE THE EXACT SIZE YOU NEED FOR THE BOTTOM. IT SHOULD FIT INSIDE THE OTHER PIECES. CUT IT OUT AND NAIL IT IN PLACE.

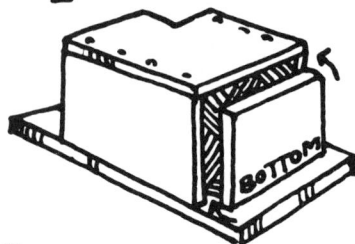

7. SET THE TOP ON AND FASTEN THE HINGES. THEY CAN BE NAILED ON, BUT SCREWS ARE BETTER. PREDRILL HOLES JUST A LITTLE BIT SMALLER THAN THE SCREWS.

8. DRILL TWO SMALL HOLES JUST UNDER THE ROOF ON EACH SIDE FOR VENTILATION. ALSO DRILL FOUR SMALL HOLES IN THE FLOOR FOR DRAINAGE IN CASE WATER GETS INSIDE.

9. YOU CAN PAINT THE OUTSIDE, BUT IT ISN'T NECESSARY. USE A NATURAL COLOUR AND DON'T PAINT THE INSIDE!

10. FASTEN THE HOUSE TO A TREE, 3 – 5 METRES ABOVE THE GROUND. THE BOTTOM CAN REST ON A BRANCH FOR SUPPORT. BE SURE IT'S A SHADY SPOT SO THE SUN CAN'T SHINE ON IT AND MAKE THE INSIDE TOO HOT.

Creatures of the Night

Animals have two worlds they can live in, a day world and a night world. Since people are mostly day animals, they see other day animals such as squirrels and birds. Night animals can live all around us without our ever seeing them, unless we know the secrets of how to look for them.

Night animals wake up in the early evening. As the sun is going down, they begin their evening journeys to look for food and water. All animals are creatures of habit. They take the same paths night after night. A fox that finds a good source of food or water will show up there at about the same time every night. Once you know where animals are likely to be, and when, it'll be easier to watch them.

Foxes live in dens in the ground. Look for holes about 20–25cm wide with a fan shape of earth beside. Fox tracks are like a dog's but narrower. Look in the mud around any kind of water, including ditches and puddles.

Rabbits also live in holes in the ground. However, you will usually see many similar holes nearby as rabbits live in colonies (warrens). On waste ground and in parks you may find well-worn paths in tall grass and at the edges of bushes. Hedgehogs, cats and other mammals besides rabbits may use these trails, so look for tracks in dust or mud to figure out which animals are using the trail.

HEDGEHOG

HEDGEHOG TRACKS

FOX TRACKS

Bats live in attics, under loose roof tiles, behind shutters, in the towers of churches, and in other dark, quiet places. Some kinds roost among the leaves of trees or in caves. Bats begin feeding just after sunset. Look for them over gardens and parks and near street lights and lighted signs that attract insects. Bats have a more erratic flight than birds. They zigzag a lot as they chase and catch insects in the air. Bats use sound waves to locate their prey. When a bat squeaks, the sound bounces off objects such as flying insects, and the bat's sensitive ears pick up the returning sound, which tells the bat where the insects are. You might hear a bat squeaking, but most of the sounds they make are too high for people to hear.

Feral cats sit sleeping under a bush or in a secluded sunny spot during the day. They also make trails through tall grass where they hunt mice and voles. A feral cat's den may be under a building or in any small, cave-like place under piles of rubbish, wood, or rocks. Look for small tracks without claw marks. (Cats retract their claws to keep them sharp for climbing trees, while dogs use theirs for traction when walking and running.)

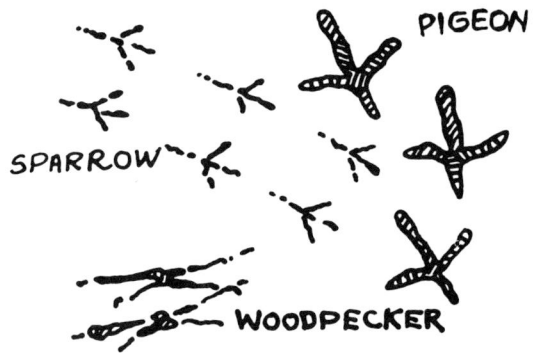

Owls roost in trees. Barn owls will roost and nest inside empty buildings or towers. Towns with large, wooded parks may have tawny owls that nest in hollow trees. The fields around airports and town edges are hunting grounds for owls, and sometimes little owls nest there. Since the good roosting and nesting spots for owls are usually in one part of town and the good hunting grounds are somewhere else, owls may fly over densely populated areas as they "commute" back and forth. Look for them in the evening, just after sunset, but while the sky is still light.

Listen for barn owl calls, a long shriek. If you hear a sharp 'ke-wick' or a deep-throated "Hoo hoo hoo," it's probably a tawny owl.

An owl can't digest the hair and bones of the animals it eats, so it compresses them and spits them up in the form of a pellet. Look for an owl roost wherever you find several pellets.

10
A BREATH OF FRESH AIR

Fresh air is something most people take for granted. We open the window and there it is, but increasingly more often fresh air isn't always fresh. Cars, factories, and other inventions of people pollute our air, especially in and near cities. Sometimes the pollution in the air becomes so bad that in certain cities people are even told to close their windows and stay indoors. In some towns people are told not to drive their cars unless absolutely necessary. We are finally realizing how much pollution we cause and worrying about spoiling our fresh air.

The Air Cycle

Oxygen is made by plants and used by animals. Carbon dioxide is made by animals and used by plants. Before there were plants on earth, there wasn't enough oxygen for animals to breathe.

Plants give off oxygen in the process called "photosynthesis." *Photo* means "light" and *synthesis* means "putting together." In photosynthesis, plants use light energy to put together their food from carbon dioxide (from the air) and water. Animals and people depend on plants to provide them with food and oxygen.

Much of our oxygen is made by trees, grass, and other land plants. Much more is made in the ocean by a group of plants called "algae." Winds carry this oxygen to land where land animals, including people, can use it. Winds also blow polluted air out over the water where it can affect the ocean. More pollution reaches the ocean through rivers and streams. We used to think of ocean waters as a good dumping place for sewage and factory wastes, but many scientists are now certain that it's dangerous to dump things there. Pollution of lakes and bays has already upset the balance of plant and animal life in many places. If we upset this balance in the ocean as well, we may affect not only the fish that feed us, but also the algae that produce most of our oxygen.

Wind

The areas around buildings are usually very windy. Did you ever leave home on a calm, sunny day and go into town to find that it was really windy? Buildings have a strong influence on wind, especially when it's warm and sunny.

First of all, when wind blows from far away across open spaces and suddenly meets buildings, it has to take a detour. Since it can't go through them, it blows around and between them. This means that a lot of air is pouring through small spaces. It's especially noticeable around buildings that have arches or short tunnels in them. You may be walking along, not paying any attention to a gentle breeze, then when you go by the entrance to a tunnel, suddenly your hat blows off.

Another reason that cities are windy has to do with the heating and cooling of the buildings and pavement. When the sun shines on buildings and pavement, they get warm and this warms the air around them. The warm air is light and begins to rise. Around the corner, the building is casting a shadow. This area is cooler than the sunny side, and this cool air is heavier. As the warm, light air on one side lifts up, it pulls the cool heavier air towards it. This movement creates a local breeze. The same principle explains air movement everywhere. In the country, air is heated by warm land and bodies of water. Find out more about the peculiar local winds around buildings with two instruments that are easy to make: an anemometer and a wind vane.

Anemometer

Meteorologists, people who study weather, use anemometers to measure wind speed in miles or kilometers per hour. You can use yours to compare the revolutions per minute (RPM) of wind in different places. All anemometer measurements are based on RPMs. When a meteorologist's anemometer turns, it measures the wind speed on a gauge, which translates the revolutions per minute into kilometres or miles per hour.

What Causes Smog and Where Does It Go?

The word "smog" is a combination of the words "smoke" and "fog." The smoke is the particles and gases given off by factories, cars, and fireplaces. The fog part is a thin mist of water

MAKE AN ANEMOMETER

YOU NEED

A BOARD 15 CM SQUARE (LARGER IS OKAY)
4 SMALL PAPER CUPS
1 PLASTIC STRAW
A STAPLER AND STAPLES
MASKING TAPE
A SQUARE OF CORRUGATED CARDBOARD 15 CM SQUARE (YOU CAN CUT THIS OUT OF A GROCERY BOX.)
1 LARGE NAIL AND A HAMMER

1. POUND THE NAIL THROUGH THE MIDDLE OF THE BOARD. (IT'S EASY TO DO IF YOU PUT THE BOARD OVER A CAN.)

2. PUNCH A HOLE IN THE CENTRE OF THE CARDBOARD SQUARE WITH THE NAIL.

3. SLIDE THE STRAW OVER THE NAIL.

4. PUSH THE STRAW INTO THE HOLE IN THE CARDBOARD AND SECURE IT WITH TAPE.

5. STAPLE THE CUPS TO THE CARDBOARD SO THEY ALL FACE THE SAME DIRECTION, AS IN DRAWING.

6. MARK AN X ON ONE CUP AND ON ONE CORNER OF THE BOARD.

COUNT ONE RPM EACH TIME THE X CUP PASSES THE X ON THE BOARD. TRY THIS IN SEVERAL PLACES—NEAR BUILDINGS, AWAY FROM BUILDINGS, IN ARCHES, AND IN TUNNELS.

RPM IS REVOLUTIONS PER MINUTE.

droplets in the air. You can think of fog as a cloud that's close to the ground.

Smog causes our eyes to itch and burn and can cause people difficulty in breathing. This is because smog contains more carbon dioxide and poisonous gases than fresh air. Breathing

MAKE A PARTICLE TRAP

YOU NEED:

A WHITE PLATE, A SHALLOW GLASS DISH, OR A MICROSCOPE SLIDE.
VASELINE
A HAND LENS OR MAGNIFYING GLASS

1. SMEAR THE GLASS WITH VASELINE.

2. SET IT OUTSIDE ON YOUR WINDOWSILL.

3. LEAVE IT THERE FOR A WEEK.

4. USE THE MAGNIFYING GLASS TO SEE THE PARTICLES YOU HAVE CAUGHT FROM THE ATMOSPHERE.

HOW TO SNAP A RUBBER BAND

NATURAL RUBBER IS SLOWLY DESTROYED BY OZONE AND OTHER GASES IN POLLUTED AIR.

YOU NEED:

RUBBER BANDS
A COAT HANGER
A CLEAN JAR WITH A LID

1. BEND THE COAT HANGER LIKE THIS - SO IT WILL HOLD SEVERAL RUBBER BANDS STRETCHED TIGHT.

2. SLIDE ON SEVERAL RUBBER BANDS.

3. HANG IT UP IN A SHADY PLACE (SUNLIGHT WILL ALSO AFFECT RUBBER).

4. PUT SEVERAL MORE OF THE RUBBER BANDS IN A JAR AND SEAL IT WITH THE LID. KEEP IT INDOORS IN A DRAWER.

5. WAIT A WEEK, THEN EXAMINE YOUR RUBBER BANDS FOR CRACKS AND BREAKS USING A MAGNIFYING GLASS. COMPARE THEM WITH THE RUBBER BANDS YOU KEPT IN A JAR BY STRETCHING THEM THE SAME AMOUNT.

6. IF THE RUBBER IS STILL IN GOOD CONDITION, CONTINUE THE EXPERIMENT FOR SEVERAL MORE WEEKS. WHERE THE AIR IS ESPECIALLY POLLUTED, RUBBER BANDS WILL SNAP IN ONE OR TWO WEEKS.

smog is bad for our health. It especially hurts people who are old or sick and those who normally have trouble breathing. Even plants are affected. Spinach can't be grown in smoggy areas because the leaves turn brown. All of the lichens in some cities have died because of smog.

The smoggiest days are warm, quiet ones when there isn't any wind. A cold layer of air called an "inversion layer" traps the warm air below it. The smog can't rise into the cold air, and on a smoggy day you can usually see a distinct edge where the warm, dirty air stops and the cold, clean air begins.

Smog is blown away when the wind is strong; rain also washes smog out of the air. And, of course, the particles that were in the smoggy air usually end up being washed into the ocean. This is why it's important for factories to cut down the amount of smoke they give off and for car companies to produce engines with cleaner exhaust. We can all help cut down on smog by riding bikes, walking, and using public transportation.

HOW TO MAKE A WIND VANE

THIS DEVICE SHOWS IN WHICH DIRECTION THE WIND IS BLOWING.

YOU NEED:
A BOARD
A LARGE NAIL AND A HAMMER

A PLASTIC STRAW

A STAPLER AND STAPLES

A STRIP OF HEAVY PAPER 1 CM BY 7 CM.

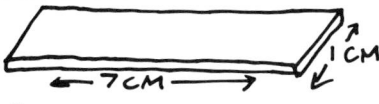

1 CM
← 7 CM →

1. HAMMER THE NAIL THROUGH THE BOARD.

2. SLIDE THE STRAW OVER THE NAIL.

3. STAPLE THE PAPER TO THE STRAW.

4. CHECK THE WIND DIRECTION IN A CLEAR, OPEN SPACE FIRST, THEN TRY IT ON DIFFERENT SIDES OF YOUR HOUSE AND ON OTHER BUILDINGS.

5. IF YOU HAVE A COMPASS, YOU CAN NAME THE ACTUAL DIRECTION THE WIND IS BLOWING FROM. HOLD THE COMPASS SO THE ARROW POINTS NORTH AND COMPARE IT WITH YOUR WIND VANE.

WIND IS NAMED FOR THE DIRECTION IT COMES FROM.

11
WHERE DOES THE RAIN GO?

All plants and animals, including humans, depend on water. We need water to drink and to wash things. A lot of animals live near streams and ponds and travel to the water every day so they can drink and wash. Some plants like to grow with their roots in the water. They need lots of water and grow where their roots will always be wet. Other plants and animals live right in the water. Some, such as frogs, spend part of their lives under the water and part on land.

The Water Cycle

All of the water we use has been used before and will be used again many times. Rain falls on the earth, seeps into the soil, flows into springs, trickles into streams, runs into rivers, and gushes into the sea. Trees and other plants drink water from the soil and move it up into their leaves. Water evaporates from leaves, soil, rivers, lakes, and oceans, forming water vapour in the air. The air cools and the water vapour condenses into clouds. Wind carries the clouds to new places, from the ocean to the land, up over mountains and cities. The clouds cool some more and it rains. This is the water cycle. Powered by the sun and wind, it moves water from the places where it collects, such as the ocean and large lakes, and returns it to other parts of the earth. All life on land depends on this movement and cycling of water.

Drinking Water for Cities

Cities use a lot of water. People drink it; we use it to wash our dishes and our bodies; we even use it in toilets to wash away our body wastes; and factories and power plants use enormous amounts of water. How do cities get enough water for all these uses?

Some cities dig wells for water. Rain water that seeps into the ground gets stored in a porous layer of rock or soil called an "aquifer." A well is drilled down into the aquifer, then the water is pumped up to the surface.

Some cities get their water from rivers or lakes. Many years ago, when these natural sources of water were clean, this water could be used directly. Now most of our rivers and lakes are polluted. This happens because factory wastes and sewage water are dumped into rivers to be carried away. The problem is that the water then flows past other cities on its way to the sea. Each city adds polluting wastes that make the water unsafe to drink. In some places the problem is so serious that fish and other river animals die as a result of this pollution. Today, river and lake water is filtered to remove waste particles and specially treated to kill germs. If your water tastes like a swimming pool, it's because a lot of chlorine has to be added to make it safe to drink.

Reservoirs are another source of city water. A dam is built across a stream or river and a reservoir or artificial lake is formed behind it. A reservoir may be many miles away from the city that uses its water. The cities of Liverpool, Manchester, and Birmingham, for example, use water from reservoirs high in the mountains of Wales. The water travels mostly in underground pipes to reach the cities.

To find out where your water comes from, call your local water authority and ask. You can look up the telephone number in the telephone book. You can also call the town hall and ask someone there. Some water authorities have free pamphlets that tell all about the water supply, and some will give talks to groups if you arrange for it in advance.

Sewage and Where It Goes

After we use water, it becomes sewage. What to do with the sewage is a big problem. Most cities don't really know what to do with it. There are actually three kinds of used water.

1. Sink and bath water isn't very dirty and could easily be cleaned if it could be kept separate from the other two kinds.

2. Toilet water contains sewage that has human germs in it that can cause people to get very sick if it isn't cleaned before it's used again.

3. Industrial water has chemicals in it from factory wastes. Environmental laws limit the amount of wastes that factories can put into water, but there is still more that could be done.

Since it's difficult to clean our water once we've dumped sewage into it, you might wonder why we don't do something else with our wastes. There are several alternatives to putting wastes into water, but it's very hard to change something everybody already does.

There are many kinds of sewage treatment; preliminary, primary, secondary, and tertiary.

Preliminary treatment passes the water through screens, which remove any hard objects which might block water pipes.

Primary treatment removes most of the solids and makes the sludge in the water settle.

Secondary treatment removes the solids, then uses natural bacteria and chemicals to further clean the water. This water becomes cleaner after it is diluted by river or sea water and after continued action by natural processes. You must not swim in or drink water that has only had secondary treatment where it comes out of the sewage treatment plant.

Tertiary treatment is the best. It goes several steps beyond secondary treatment to clean the water so you can drink it or swim in it. By the time sewage treatment is finished, every drop of water supplied to your house is clean enough to drink.

Visit a Sewage Treatment Plant

Some sewage treatment plants give tours. You can call the one nearest to you to ask if they do. It will help if you want the tour for an organized group such as a club, scout troup, or school class. Sewage treatment plants usually belong to the local water authority and are listed that way in the phone book. It's funny how people try to avoid using the words "sewage" and "rubbish." Sewage treatment plants become "treatment plants" and rubbish dumps become "land reclamation sites." If you have trouble finding your local sewage treatment plant, call your town hall for information.

Saving Water

Every year people use more and more water. We let it run down our drains, flush through our toilets, pour out of hoses in our gardens, and go to waste in our factories. Water is expensive, but not just because of what we have to pay the water company when we receive the bill. Water costs us miles and miles of beautiful, wild rivers and valleys every time a dam is built. Water costs us animals, such as the minnow, that live in streams but can't survive in the new reservoirs. When we save water, we help to save these natural elements.

You can save water by turning off the tap while you brush your teeth and wash your hands. You can save by using water twice. When you wash vegetables, catch the water in a bucket. Then use that water to water plants. Think of how you can save water when you water a garden, wash a car, and bathe.

In California there was a severe drought that lasted for two years. Even very little children learned that we don't have to flush the toilet every time we use it. Many people put a brick in the toilet tank so that each flush would use a little less water. People were surprised to find out just how much water they could save. Many of them used less than half as much as they'd used before. When you call your water authority to find out where your water comes from, ask them about how to save water.

Puddles and Other Wet Places

Between the time water falls out of the sky and the time it evaporates into the air and forms clouds, it is a home for many living things.

Animals that live in water can be found almost everywhere: in puddles, ditches, drains, old tyres, and bottles, as well as in streams and lakes. Wherever water has been sitting around for a while, something is likely to be at home there. Of course, small things live in small places. You wouldn't expect to find a shark in an old tyre, but you might find water fleas, mosquito larvae, or even a small water beetle.

After it rains, go outside and see what you can find that has been filled with water. Keep checking to see if something starts to live there. A greenish colour will mean that algae are starting to grow. Look for tiny things the size of pinheads swimming around. These will probably be water fleas, seed shrimp, or cyclops. The longer the water stays, the more creatures will have a chance to start living there.

You might wonder how something can start living in a puddle when nothing was there before. Tiny animals such as water fleas have tiny eggs that lie in the soil waiting for rain. The eggs were laid the last time there was a puddle, or perhaps they were picked up with dust and blown there by the wind. Other animals such as water boatmen and water beetles can fly from puddle to puddle.

LIFE IN A PUDDLE

HERE ARE SOME OF THE ANIMALS YOU MIGHT FIND LIVING IN PUDDLES.

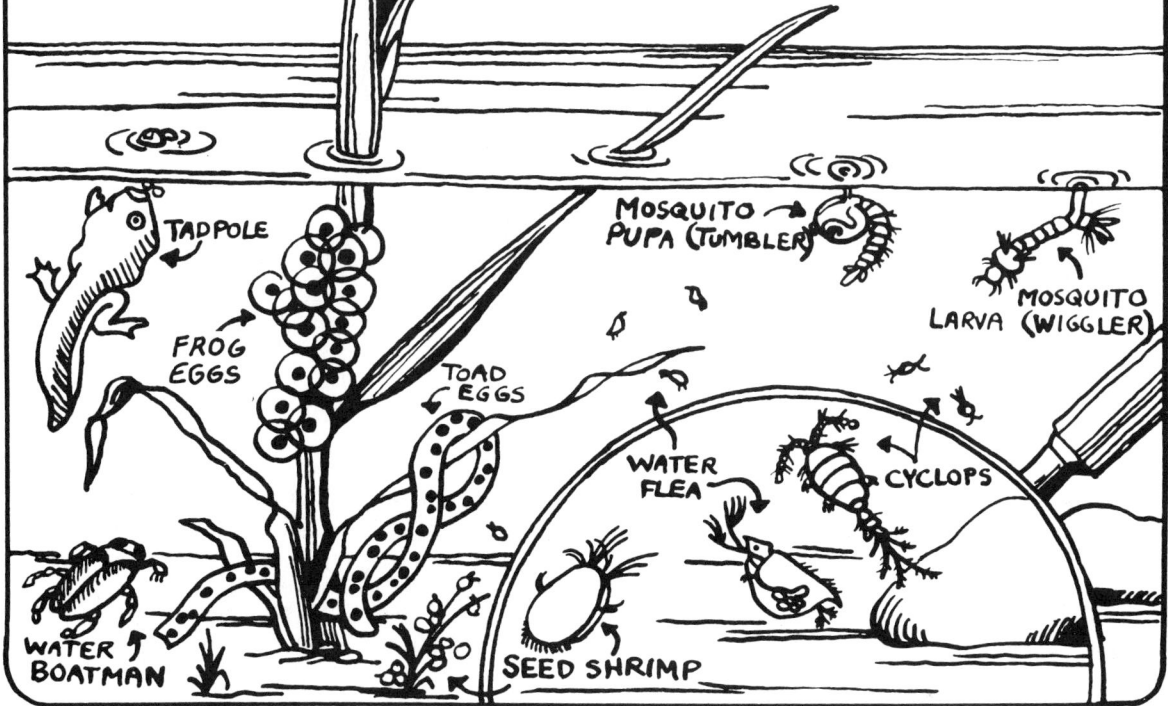

TADPOLE

FROG EGGS

TOAD EGGS

MOSQUITO PUPA (TUMBLER)

MOSQUITO LARVA (WIGGLER)

WATER FLEA

CYCLOPS

WATER BOATMAN

SEED SHRIMP

Life in a Puddle

Here are some of the animals you might find living in puddles: water boatmen, mosquito larvae (wigglers), mosquito pupae (tumblers), water fleas, seed shrimp, cyclops, tadpoles, toad eggs, and frog eggs.

Water boatmen are true bugs that live *in* the water. They eat algae and breathe air. Watch them hide in the mud at the bottom of a puddle. Then wait a minute and watch them come up for air. True bugs are insects that have leathery wings, which can be folded. They also have sucking mouthparts. Other true bugs you might see are pond skaters.

Cyclops, water fleas, and seed shrimp are tiny crustaceans that live in water everywhere. You can watch them best if you put them in a jar with some algae or sticks from the puddle. Hold the jar up to the light and watch them swim. These animals use their antennae like oars to row through the water. A magnifying glass will help you see all the action.

Mosquitoes lay their eggs in

HOW TO MAKE YOUR OWN PUDDLE

SINCE ALMOST ANYTHING THAT HOLDS WATER CAN BE A PUDDLE, IT'S VERY EASY TO MAKE YOUR OWN.

OUTDOOR PUDDLES

1. FILL JARS, AN OLD TYRE, OR A BUCKET WITH WATER.

2. PUT LEAVES, STONES, AND A STICK OR TWO IN THE WATER.

3. PUT YOUR PUDDLE IN A SHADY PLACE WHERE IT WON'T BE DISTURBED.

4. HAVE PATIENCE AND KEEP YOUR PUDDLES FILLED. IT TAKES A WHILE FOR ANIMALS TO FIND A NEW PUDDLE.

NOTE: YOU CAN HELP YOUR PUDDLE GET STARTED BY ADDING PLANTS AND ANIMALS FROM OTHER PUDDLES.

INDOOR PUDDLES

1. FIND AN OUTDOOR PUDDLE AND PUT WATER AND A FEW ANIMALS AND PLANTS FROM IT INTO A LARGE JAR. PUDDLE ALGAE WILL LOOK LIKE GREEN STRINGS OR A MUDDY GREEN MAT. IF YOU USE LOTS OF ALGAE AND A FEW ANIMALS, YOUR INDOOR PUDDLE WILL FEED AND CARE FOR ITSELF.

2. ADD A LITTLE PUDDLE WATER WHEN THE WATER LEVEL GETS LOW (OR ADD TAP WATER AND LET IT SIT IN A PAN OVERNIGHT TO GET RID OF THE CHLORINE).

3. TADPOLES WILL NEED TO BE FED. GIVE YOUNG TADPOLES ALGAE, LETTUCE, OR SPINACH. GIVE OLDER TADPOLES SMALL CRUSTACEANS OR TINY BITS OF RAW LIVER OR HAMBURGER. THEY SHOULD HAVE SOMETHING TO CLIMB OUT ON WHEN THEY DEVELOP LEGS. THEIR WATER WILL NEED TO BE CHANGED WHEN YOU FEED THEM MEAT.

1. LET TAP WATER SIT IN A JAR OVERNIGHT TO GET RID OF THE CHLORINE.

2. FIND A DITCH OR A DRIED-UP PUDDLE AND DIG SOME SOIL AND DRIED ALGAE FROM ITS BOTTOM.

INSTANT PUDDLES

IF IT'S TOO DRY OUTSIDE FOR PUDDLES, YOU CAN MAKE ONE.

3. PUT THIS "INSTANT PUDDLE MIX" IN THE JAR OF WATER AND WAIT.

4. IN ABOUT A WEEK YOU WILL BE ABLE TO SEE WHAT YOU DUG UP. SOMETIMES INSTANT PUDDLES ARE FULL OF WATER FLEAS, SEED SHRIMP, OR CYCLOPS. IF YOU'RE LUCKY, YOU'LL FIND ALL THREE.

little rafts on the surface of the water. The eggs hatch into wigglers, or larvae, which eat microscopic plants. The tumblers, or pupae, are in a resting stage that's similar to the cocoon stage of moths. Tumblers don't eat, but they do breathe air. Watch them hanging just at the surface of the water, and you'll see the little breathing tubes they use. Watch wigglers and tumblers and you'll see how they got their common names.

Tadpoles grow up to be frogs or toads. They hatch from eggs, and it's difficult to tell whether they're toads or frogs until they've grown. Most toads lay their eggs in strings. Most frogs lay eggs in clumps or singly attached to plants. Young tadpoles eat algae and other plants. Older tadpoles, which have legs, begin eating meat in the form of mosquito larvae, water fleas, cyclops, and seed shrimp.

12
THROW THAT AWAY!

Wait! Wait! Maybe you can do something else with it. After all, air is recycled, and so is water. In fact, in the natural world, almost everything is used over and over again. There must be a reason for that.

People are just beginning to learn about the importance of recycling, but many of our animal and plant neighbours have known about it all along. They are natural recyclers. Did you know that your rubbish is someone else's dinner, at least it can be if it isn't sent to the rubbish dump, burned, or buried too deep in the ground. Think about what you throw away after a meal. There might be potato peels, a few leftover vegetables, some apple cores, and a crust of bread. Outside, living among the leaves, there are worms, springtails, woodlice, and a host of other animals that will eat these things. They're the same creatures you met on your "Expedition to an Old Board." These animals, along with moulds and other fungi, turn leftovers into compost, and compost is good food for plants. Compost makes them grow faster and larger and keeps them healthy. When a plant grows, it removes minerals from the soil. These minerals become part of the plant until it dies and is recycled by soil animals. If the plant is harvested, the minerals from the dead plant aren't returned to the soil. Adding compost to soil is a way of giving back some of the minerals so the healthy new plants can grow.

Of course, not all rubbish is food. Bottles, cans, and plastic can't be eaten by anything, but it's important to recycle what we can. By recycling glass, iron, and aluminum we save energy and also reduce litter. Plastic is a problem. It can't be recycled either by people or soil animals. Because it doesn't break down easily, plastic rubbish will be around for a long time. The only thing we can do is use as little plastic as possible and encourage manufacturers to develop plastics that can be recycled.

How to Produce Less Rubbish

Making less rubbish begins with how you think about things. Years ago, people recycled things automatically. Food

wasn't already in packages when it was bought from a shop. People bought pickles from a crock, fish from a barrel, and vegetables from a bin. Could you think of another example? Today meat, biscuits, and even tomatoes come wrapped in paper and plastic. At

one time hardware shops had boxes and drawers filled with nails, screws, and other items. Today these hang on display racks in little packages of plastic. It takes some hunting to find a shop that will sell nails the old-fashioned way. You can still buy meat from a butcher who cuts it for you and wraps it in paper instead of plastic, and you can still find vegetables that aren't wrapped in plastic. When we pack our groceries in our own cloth bags and buy groceries that aren't packaged, we are helping to produce less rubbish. Your head is saying. "If I don't buy rubbish, I won't have rubbish to get rid of."

Suppose you've had to buy the rubbish anyway. After all, milk often comes in cartons now and the dairy just isn't **going to recycle all those cartons. This is where your mind has to be inventive. How are you going to use all those milk cartons, egg cartons, and coffee cans again? The more things you can reuse, the fewer things you'll have to throw away.**

Things You Can Do with Rubbish

Glass, aluminium, steel, and paper can all be recycled. In some cities, recycling centres have been set up to collect these things and transport them to companies that can reuse them.

You may have to do some telephoning to find out how to recycle. Your local ecology centre, town hall, newspaper, scout headquarters, or librarian should be able to help you. When you see someone collecting aluminium tins, ask them where they take them. Aluminium can be sold to tin or drink companies, and some people make extra money this way.

Milk-Carton Boats

In the United States of America the State Milk Advisory Boards sponsor milk-carton boat races. The boats use milk cartons for flotation and decoration. They hold one or more people, who use paddles to speed them over the

110

water. Contestants wear life jackets, and rescue crews stand by in case a boat comes apart.

There are many possible designs for milk-carton boats. Most have a rigid frame made out of wood. The boats float by resting on a cushion of air trapped inside empty milk cartons. The cartons are resealed to make them watertight and are held in the frame with string or tape. It takes 40 two-litre milk cartons to float one person. Some boats have teams of five or six people, so you can imagine how many milk cartons have to be saved from the rubish.

Before you build a boat, you could find out if there's a local race and what the rules are. Meanwhile you can build a small model to see how it works.

Containers and Canisters

Tins can be covered with paint, decorated paper, or cloth to make interesting containers. A soup tin may become a pencil holder, a tuna tin might become a jewel box, and a coffee tin with its plastic lid can become a biscuit tin. Think of all the things you have that could be stored in decorated tins: crayons, marbles, clay, small trucks, doll clothes, and building blocks to name a few.

A MILK-CARTON BOAT

YOU NEED:
6 TO 10 MILK CARTONS
PARAFFIN (WAX)
AN OLD COFFEE TIN
STRONG WATERPROOF TAPE
A STAPLER AND STAPLES

1. MELT THE PARAFFIN BY PUTTING IT IN THE COFFEE TIN AND PUTTING THE COFFEE TIN IN A PAN OF HOT WATER ON THE STOVE. (GET HELP FROM AN ADULT FOR THIS PART.)

2. STAPLE EACH CARTON CLOSED AND DIP INTO THE MELTED PARAFFIN.

3. TAPE THE MILK CARTONS TOGETHER WITH STRONG TAPE.

4. FLOAT YOUR BOAT IN YOUR BATHTUB OR ON A POND. IMAGINE HOW MANY MILK CARTONS YOU'D NEED TO BUILD A BOAT TO CARRY PEOPLE.

Plant Pots and Seed Starters

Tins, milk cartons, and egg cartons can be used as plant pots or for starting seeds. Punch holes in the bottom for drainage and fill with your own compost.

PAINT A TIN

YOU NEED:

ENAMEL PAINT
A PAINT BRUSH

PAINT THINNER TO CLEAN THE BRUSH (BE CAREFUL— PAINT THINNER IS POISONOUS, SO HAVE AN ADULT HELP WITH THIS PART.)

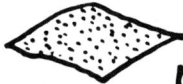

FINE SANDPAPER

NEWSPAPER TO PUT UNDER YOUR WORK.

1. ROUGH UP THE TIN WITH FINE SANDPAPER SO THE PAINT WILL STICK TO IT.

2. DUST OFF THE TIN AFTER SANDING.

3. PAINT THE TIN WITH A LIGHT COAT OF PAINT.

4. SOME TINS WILL NEED TWO COATS OF PAINT. FOLLOW THE DIRECTIONS ON THE PAINT TIN FOR DRYING TIME BETWEEN COATS OF PAINT.

5. CLEAN YOUR BRUSH. (HAVE AN ADULT HELP.)

COVER A TIN

YOU NEED:

PAPER OR CLOTH TO GO AROUND YOUR TIN

CRAYONS OR MARKING PENS

SCISSORS

CLEAR TAPE

1. CUT THE MATERIAL SO THAT IT FITS AROUND THE TIN WITH A LITTLE BIT LEFT OVER.

2. IF YOU USE PAPER, YOU CAN DRAW OR COLOUR A DESIGN ON IT.

3. TAPE THE MATERIAL AROUND THE TIN.

HOW MANY USES CAN YOU FIND FOR COVERED TINS?

RUBBISH FANTASIES

EGG CARTONS, MILK CARTONS, AND CARDBOARD BOXES CAN BE USED TO BUILD HOUSES, FARMS, SPACE STATIONS, ROCKET SHIPS, AND DOLL HOUSES. THERE AREN'T ANY RULES FOR MAKING THESE THINGS, YOU JUST USE YOUR IMAGINATION. YOU NEED CARTONS AND CARDBOARD BOXES THAT CAN BE CUT UP, STRONG SCISSORS, AND LOTS OF MASKING TAPE.

NOTE: IT'S ALSO NICE TO HAVE FABRIC AND FOAM SCRAPS TO MAKE FURNITURE, AND FELT TIP PENS TO DRAW DETAILS SUCH AS WINDOWS, LETTERS, AND INSTRUMENT PANELS. HAVE FUN!

HOW TO MAKE COMPOST

FOOD RUBBISH CAN BECOME FERTILIZER FOR YOUR PLANTS. YOU WILL NEED A PLASTIC DUSTBIN. WITH A LID, SOIL, SOIL ANIMALS, DECAYING LEAVES, A KNIFE, VEGETABLE RUBBISH. (MEAT AND BONES WILL ATTRACT RATS, SO DON'T USE THEM.)

1. CUT SMALL HOLES IN THE DUSTBIN LID WITH THE KNIFE. THEY SHOULD LET IN AIR BUT NOT FLIES. FLY LARVAE (MAGGOTS) ARE RECYCLERS, TOO, BUT FLIES CAN SPREAD DISEASES, SO YOU DON'T WANT THEM.

2. PUT SOME SOIL IN THE BOTTOM OF THE BIN.

3. ADD SOME VEGETABLE RUBBISH. THERE SHOULD BE AS MUCH SOIL AS RUBBISH WHEN YOU'RE STARTING.

4. ADD DECAYING LEAVES. THESE WILL BRING MOULDS AND OTHER FUNGI TO YOUR COMPOST AND HELP IT GET STARTED.

5. ADD SOIL ANIMALS. SPRINGTAILS, WORMS, AND WOODLICE ARE GOOD.

6. STIR YOUR COMPOST WITH A STICK. COMPOST SHOULD BE DAMP BUT NOT WET. SPRINKLE WITH WATER OR ADD DRY SOIL OR SAWDUST TO KEEP THE MOISTURE RIGHT.

7. PUT THE BIN OUTDOORS. IN COLD WEATHER, LET IT WARM UP IN THE SUN. IN HOT WEATHER PROTECT YOUR SOIL ANIMALS FROM GETTING TOO HOT BY MOVING THE BIN INTO THE SHADE.

8. EVERY DAY WHEN YOU ADD MORE VEGETABLE RUBBISH, ALSO ADD A SPRINKLING OF SOIL AND STIR IT. (CHOP YOUR RUBBISH INTO SMALL PIECES TO GET IT TO COMPOST FASTER.)

9. WHEN THE BIN IS ¾ FULL OR GETS HARD TO STIR, STOP ADDING RUBBISH AND LET IT WORK. IN 3 TO 6 WEEKS YOU WILL HAVE FINISHED COMPOST FOR PLANTS. IF YOU HAVE TWO BINS, YOU CAN ALWAYS HAVE ONE STARTING WHILE ONE FINISHES.

COMPOST IS GOOD FOR HOUSE PLANTS, GARDEN PLANTS, TREES, AND TERRARIUMS. NATURAL COMPOST IS EXPENSIVE TO BUY AT THE SHOP SO IT MAKES A NICE PRESENT FOR PEOPLE WHO HAVE GARDENS.

13
ISLANDS IN A CONCRETE SEA

Parks are refuges for the animals of cities and towns. In areas where there are many buildings, they may be the last places where the original inhabitants can still survive. Some big parks are homes for foxes, rabbits, hawks, owls, and other animals, which would have to live miles from the city if the parks didn't exist. Rare butterflies, and flowers are sometimes discovered living in parks, while all around them their natural habitat is covered over with buildings and pavement.

The happiest parks are those that are allowed to be a little wild. Places with streams or natural water are often left this way. The saddest parks are those where the grass is always mowed, the hedges trimmed, and the trees pruned.

Park habitats may be large or small. Fields and woods will probably have some of the same animals that live in the country. A marshy place with reeds may be a home for many marsh animals, including some rare ones.

Small park habitats are interesting too. Mini-habitats include shrubs, trees, leaves, and petals of flowers. The drama of a crab spider stalking a fly on a rose petal can be just as exciting as that of a hawk diving for a mouse.

exploring. Look for things such as water, muddy places and puddles, weedy places, piles of leaves, or places where there is a thick layer of leaves on the ground. Find dead trees, stones that can be turned over, flowers that bees visit, and bushes where spiders spin their webs. When you think you've learned where everything is, take some time to get to know one or two spots better. A good way to do this is to take some friends and play a *quiet* game there. You could also do your homework or read a book.

You can learn the most about parks by visiting a lot of different ones. Get a map of your city and find out where the parks are. Most city and town parks can be reached by bus. Take some friends along for company. It's more fun than exploring by yourself. You can start a diary of park adventure. Write a description of each one, how you got there, and what you saw. You can even write about the games you played with your friends and ask them to write in the diary too. If you like making up stories or writing poetry, you can create word images to help you remember each place.

Pick a Particular Park

The first thing to do with your park is to get to know it. Walk all the paths and then start *really*

While you are sitting there ignoring them, the birds and other animals will have time to forget their fears and get a closer look at you. While they're watching you, you can watch them. Remember to turn your head slightly and look at animals out of the corners of your eyes. They will be less afraid because they won't think that you're a dangerous predator who wants to eat them.

Watching animals takes a lot of patience. If you wait long enough and really pay attention, you will see many things that other people miss. You may see a bird carry food to its young, watch a rabbit come out of its hole to eat grass, or observe the way a spider paralyzes and wraps an insect caught in its web.

Another way to see better is to *listen*. Your ears can give you lots of clues about what is going on around you. The best way to discover baby birds, insects, lizards, mice, and rabbits is with your ears. Twittering and cheeping, rustling leaves, and munching sounds are all clues that an animal is active nearby.

Listening Game

Try this game with your friends. Sit down in your park, close your eyes, and listen for five minutes. Let one person open his or her eyes once in a while to check a watch or clock. Five minutes can seem like a long time with your eyes closed, but the longer you sit, the more you'll hear. Listen for everything: cars, planes, birds, dogs. When the time is up, compare sounds. What did you hear? Did all of you hear the same sounds? Were there sounds you could not identify? If you want to keep score, give one point to the first person who finds the source of each sound.

Wildlife Map

Make a large map of your park. Choose a part of it where you spend a lot of time. Draw the paths, benches, large trees, and bushy areas. After the basic features are drawn, start adding animals. Every time you see a new bird, squirrel, insect, or other animal, put it on the map in the place where you saw it. You'll be surprised how quickly your map gets full. Don't worry if you don't know the names of everything you see. *You* know what the red bird and white spider are, and when you see them again, you'll remember them.

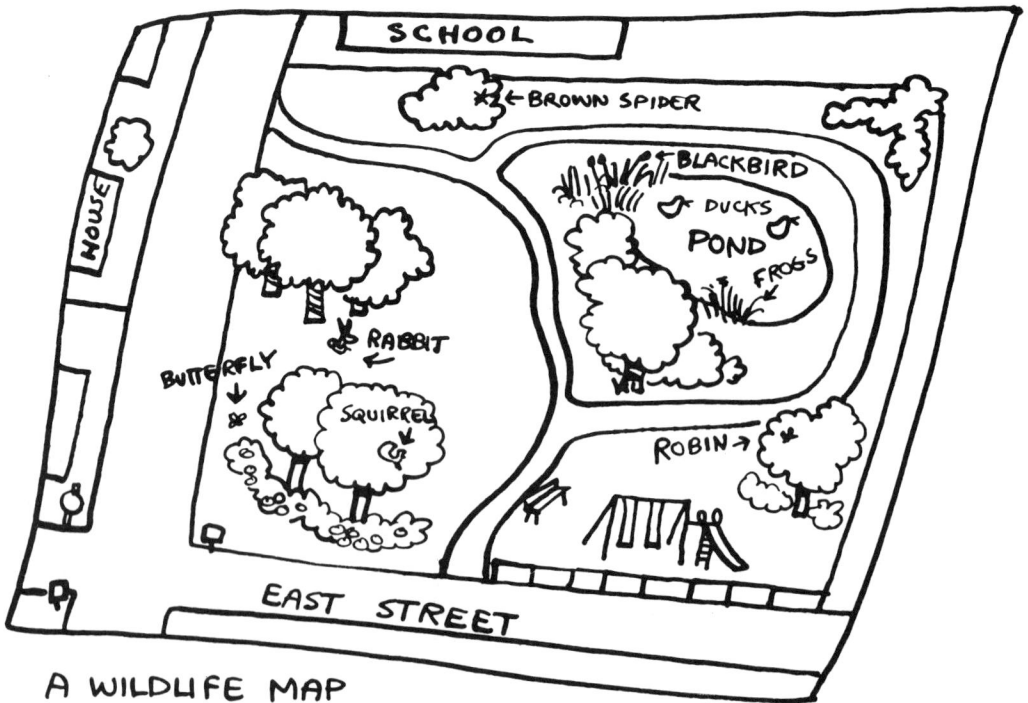

A WILDLIFE MAP

14
CITY CINDERELLA

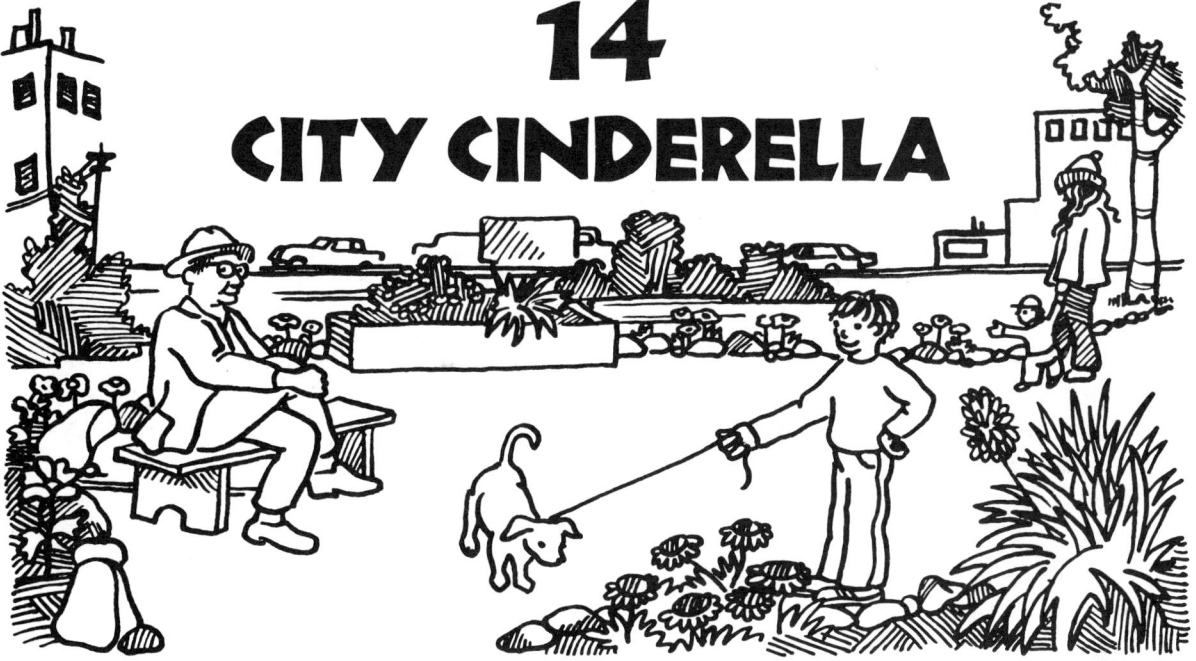

Once upon a time there was a poor miserable playground that nobody loved. A long time ago it had been paved over with tarmac and fenced with a very tall chainlink fence. In one corner there were some metal bars to climb on, and hopscotch and other game designs were painted on the tarmac. No birds, trees, or flowers lived there, but a few weeds grew around the edges where the paving was cracked. Kids spent a lot of time sitting on benches or playing games with balls. There wasn't much else to do.

This went on for a long time. Then one day some people had an idea. They didn't like the playground. They thought it was a sad, dull place, and yet they could see that it was large and had possibilities. It didn't occur to them that they were going to become fairy godmothers and fathers. All they knew was that their playground needed help and it was up to them to do something.

First they would make a plan. They needed lots of ideas from kids and their parents and the teachers. They made plans and went to work. Everybody, the kids included, drew designs and talked about what kind of place they wanted to play in. They raised money to buy what they needed, and then it was time to start.

The playground was divided into sections. One part of the paving was saved for ball games, and another area was set aside for a great maze of wooden structures to climb on. The third part was to be the nature area, and it needed a lot of work.

One day everybody pitched in and began tearing up the tarmac. New soil was brought in to form small hills, and everybody helped hollow out two big ponds. Soon it was time to plant things. The kids planted trees and flowers and grass. Around the ponds they planted reeds and rushes. Along one edge they built vegetable gardens, and beside the fence they planted climbing plants.

The kids visited wild ponds and brought back water snails, frogs, and beetles to live in their ponds. Soon birds moved into the trees, and butterflies began to visit the flowers. Fish were put in the ponds, and kids planted vegetables in the gardens.

Today it's hard to believe that there was ever tarmac where the trees are. The trees are tall, the bushes are big, and the whole nature area looks like a small forest. The ugly chainlink fence is covered with plants, and birds sit there and sing or look for insects among the leaves. The playground is still changing. As new kids and their parents come to the school, they have new ideas for it. Each new person who helps the playground becomes a fairy godmother or father to it, and as long as that happens, this City Cinderella will live happily ever after at the school.